Garden Blueprints

25 EASY-TO-FOLLOW DESIGNS FOR BEAUTIFUL LANDSCAPES

BECKE DAVIS,

HARRIET CRAMER, AND DARIA PRICE BOWMAN
ILLUSTRATIONS BY JANE KENDALL

FRIEDMAN/FAIRFAX
PUBLISHERS

A FRIEDMAN/FAIRFAX BOOK
Friedman/Fairfax Publishers
15 West 26 Street
New York, NY 10010
Telephone (212) 685-6610
Fax (212) 685-1307
Please visit our website: www.metrobooks.com

Library of Congress Cataloging-in-Publication Data available upon request.

ISBN 1-58663-041-5

Editor: Susan Lauzau
Art Director: Jeff Batzli
Photography Editor: Deidra Gorgos
Illustrations: ©Jane Kendall
Line drawings: Amy Talluto

Color separations by Radstock Repro Ltd.
Printed in Hong Kong by Midas Printing Co. Ltd.

1 3 5 7 9 10 8 6 4 2

Distributed by Sterling Publishing Company, Inc.
387 Park Avenue South
New York, NY 10016
Distributed in Canada by Sterling Publishing
Canadian Manda Group
One Atlantic Avenue, Suite 105
Toronto, Ontario, Canada M6K 3E7
Distributed in Australia by
Capricorn Link (Australia) Pty Ltd.
P.O. Box 6651
Baulkham Hills, Business Centre, NSW 2153, Australia

Garden designs by:

Becke Davis:
Children's Curiosity Garden
Four Seasons Garden
Fragrant Garden
Moonlight Garden
Backyard Wetland
Waterwise Garden
Sunny Garden
White Garden
Raised Bed Herb Garden
Antique Rose and Heirloom Flower Garden
Medieval Pleasure Garden
Garden Rockery
Ornamental Garden of Fruits
Low-Maintenance Garden

Daria Price Bowman:
City Courtyard Garden
Hot Color Garden
Streamside Garden
Seaside Garden
Formal Vegetable Garden

Harriet Cramer:
Container Garden
Backyard Meadow Garden
Hummingbird Garden
Garden for Deep Shade
Two Cutting Gardens: For Sun and Shade

Who loves a garden

Finds within his soul

Life's whole;

He hears the anthem of the soil

While ingrates toil;

And sees beyond his little sphere

The waving fronds of heaven, clear.

LOUISE SEYMOUR JONES

Contents

Introduction

How does your garden grow? Some gardens grow plant by plant at the whim of the gardener, possibly maturing into a cohesive design but not really evolving from a specific plan. A garden that is created in such a serendipitous manner might become a work of art, but quite frequently it will end up looking like a hodgepodge of flowers and leaves. If you've ever wondered why some gardens are attractive, appealing, and soothing all at the same time while others are distracting, disorganized, and even a bit disturbing, the answer boils down to one word: design.

Successful garden designs have the same elements as beautiful paintings—good composition, balance, color, and perspective. It is also important to consider the "bones," or structure, of the garden, the form of foliage and flowers, and the use of color to create depth. "Borrowed" features such as a neighbor's fence or trees, mountains on the horizon, or even a barn in the background can be used to complement the garden and complete a view. You might wish to create a sense of mystery by adding a curving path, while tension or calm can be induced through the spatial relationships between different elements in the garden. The architecture of the house should also be reflected in the garden design, tying the garden smoothly to the house instead of making it look as if it fell into the wrong yard.

Layout is as much a part of gardening as color, even though some garden layouts are so subtly implemented that they look like the work of nature. The designs in this book can stand alone or can be adapted to tie in with an existing landscape. If your present garden is just a flat stretch of sod, the plan of your choice will be easy to adapt. If you have a mature landscape that needs renovation, see if one of the following plans can be adapted to make the most of the plants you want to save. One of the first things you'll have to do is assess your planting space and decide how many plants you'll need. Unfortunately, the number of plants required depends not only on the space available but on the habit and growth rate of each particular plant. (Is it spreading, tall and skinny, or floppy? Is it fast-growing or will it take decades to mature?) Not only that, but plants behave differently under various conditions, which makes giving a precise number of plants impractical. If you are unfamiliar with the plants you plan to grow, consult your Cooperative Extension Service (listed under county government in the phone book), local garden center, neighboring gardeners, and reference books to find out how the specific plants will fare in your area. And as with most gardening projects, expect a fair amount of experimentation to get the right effect.

Remember that gardens don't happen overnight—however closely you follow a plan. It will take a year or more for your new garden to come of age. To avoid a bare look, either purchase a few larger plants to give the impression of a mature garden or plant more than the recommended number of plants. As the plants reach their full size, dig up the extras and either give them to friends or find a new spot in your garden for them. Schools, churches, and neighbors are often more than happy to take garden "leftovers." As an alternative, you can fill your garden in with inexpensive annuals until the perennials, shrubs, and trees mature.

Gardeners today are becoming more demanding—no matter how beautifully a tree or shrub may bloom, two weeks of breathtaking blossoms cannot really justify a plant's place in the garden for the other fifty weeks of the year. Whenever possible, select plants that offer more than one season of interest in the garden. (This is subjective, though—for example, forsythia may look nondescript or even messy most of the year, but it pays for its place in the garden with the golden coin of its incomparable early spring bloom.) Look for plants with a long period of bloom, attractive form and foliage, fragrance, interesting bark, autumn color, or fruit or berries to attract wildlife. Plants with more than one ornamental talent will reward you with a garden that is beautiful throughout the seasons.

In most parts of the country, spring is considered the optimal time for planting, although many plants can be successfully transplanted in the autumn. Bulbs and peonies should be planted in autumn, while it is usually best to plant ornamental grasses in the spring. Hostas and peonies may seem to disappear over the winter, but—unless hungry wildlife ate every root—you should see the green curls of hosta and the red fronds of peony pushing up through the ground in early spring. Whatever season you plant the garden, make sure to prepare the soil. Dig at least to 6 inches (15cm) deep and preferably to 12 (30cm). Before planting, incorporate peat moss or compost. Watering is critical; for the first year at least, make sure plants get a thorough soaking at least once a week. Once the garden is established, supplemental watering may still be needed if you do not receive at least an inch of rain per week, even for plants that are drought resistant. To ensure that your plants are getting the nutrients they need, look for an organic fertilizer at your garden center and follow the manufacturer's directions.

A full season's growth is usually needed for plants to become fairly established; transplant shock may be visible in trees and shrubs any time during the first year. Prune out dead branches of trees, shrubs, and vines at planting time; trees may benefit from light pruning to balance the pruning of the roots when they were dug at the nursery. Whenever possible, select plants that have been grown locally. Be careful when substituting cultivars (for example, purchasing a familiar but disease-plagued 'Hopa' crabapple tree instead of a recommended new cultivar such as 'Donald Wyman' can be a mistake)—there may be huge differences in ultimate size and shape, hardiness, disease resistance, and ornamental qualities from one cultivar to the next.

From straightforward flower beds to more complex designs, most plans can be adapted to fit your own backyard. The beautiful illustrations make it easy to envision each garden theme—the hard part will be choosing just one. If you find a plan you love but it is not within your means, don't give up. It is perfectly possible for gardeners on a budget to install a garden section by section, working within a plan. It is also possible for a garden to start out following one design only to have it evolve into something entirely different—every garden ends up showing the "fingerprints" of the gardener. *Garden Blueprints* is both a practical guide and a book to dream over on cold winter nights. When planting time arrives the well-thumbed pages will help even novice gardeners transform their yards into unforgettable gardens.

A well-planned garden will reward the gardener year after year.

Children's Curiosity Garden

A child's garden should first and foremost be a place that appeals to kids more than to adults. The world looks different to children—grown-ups see a weed and want to yank it out. Children see dandelion clocks, lucky four-leaf clovers, amazing thistles, and blades of crabgrass thick enough to make a whistle. Children have no hesitation about smelling flowers—not by taking dainty whiffs, but by shoving their noses smack into the flower. They will pluck a handful of blossoms without a qualm. They like plants to be interesting instead of just pretty—children will be most impressed with plants that are monstrously big, unbelievably minute, sweet or smelly, spiky or soft. And children are fascinated with the birds, butterflies, and bugs that accompany the flowers as much as with the flowers themselves.

A child's garden should have something for all the senses—sweet and pungent fragrances; smooth and fuzzy textures; vivid colors; tangy or minty herbs and luscious fruits; and the tinkle of windchimes, the rattle of dry seedpods, or the rustle of tall grasses. Because children may taste things that adults would never dream of putting in their mouths, avoid plants that are poisonous to ingest—and don't even consider plants that are dangerous to touch.

Passionflower

Include plants that will attract wildlife, birds, hummingbirds, and butterflies. Bees are wonderful to watch and necessary for a healthy garden, but when children are allergic to bees or are terribly afraid of them, avoid planting flowers, such as bee balm, that are especially inviting to bees. In this plan, bee balm may be replaced with vivid pink New England asters (*Aster novae-angliae* 'Alma Potschke'); the bloom period starts later than bee balm but it lasts a long time. Usually the bees are more interested in the flowers than the kids, but don't take chances where allergies are involved.

The big blue hostas and flat, spreading mats of thyme in this design will provide fragrance as they become larger and more established, while the flowers of the PeeGee treeform hydrangea, spikes of gayfeather, and others can be easily be dried for use in nature crafts. Cup and saucer plant is a biennial and will only flower every other year, but the unusual flowers are just right to spark a child's imagination. Though the 'Horstmann's Silberlocke' Korean fir is not one you'll find at every corner nursery, it's worth the trouble to search for it. In addition to giving the garden some structure and winter interest, kids (and adults, too) will be fascinated by the tightly curled, silvery needles of this excellent cultivar. This fir will take several years to reach its full size, but remember that even if it's only four feet (1.2m) tall when you plant it, it is not a dwarf conifer.

The weeping hemlock and Harry Lauder's walking stick, with its crazily contorted branches and dangling catkins, will also add winter interest. This walking stick is intriguing but it will need some annual pruning; removing suckering branches and thinning out excess branches once in late autumn should suffice. The butterfly bush should survive most winters, and the roots will usually survive even if the top branches should die back—just prune them almost to the ground. Butterfly bushes really live up to their names, but as the flowers die the butterfly visits taper off. Cut off the spent flowers to encourage new blooms—and watch the butterflies return! The flowers of the rose of Sharon look wildly exotic, reaching up to five inches (12cm) across, but this shrub is hardy to at least Zone 5 (even further north in a protected spot). It's relatively easy to find in small containers, but remember that it will eventually grow to about eight feet (2.4m) tall and five feet (1.5m) wide.

Don't forget to include a hidden layer of bulbs. Bulbs are easy to plant and most are easy to grow (unless wildlife eat them first), and many will multiply nicely. When the flowers of bulbs are spent, let the foliage die before cutting it back. Many gardeners like to tie the foliage into a neat knot to disguise the inelegant stalks, or you can use the emergent foliage of hostas or other bushy plants to hide the dying foliage. The foliage of windflowers, crocuses, and grape hyacinth seems

Small-flowered clematis

to fade away without help, while a few—like the broad leaves of dwarf wild garlic—look good after the flowers are gone.

The tall, amazing flowers of crown imperials have been in cultivation for four centuries; once planted, they do not like to be disturbed. Why hide such aristocratic flowers at the back of the garden? Because they stink—there's no other word for it. You will think the garden has been visited by a skunk (or two); I have noticed this even before the plant is in flower, but I didn't want to identify the source of the smell badly enough to want to bring my nose closer to the foliage. The nasty scent might even be a plus in a kid's eyes ("Awesome! It's really gross!"), and it has the added benefit of—reputedly—keeping away moles and other garden pests.

Finally, there are all kinds of gardens that will appeal to kids. While this "curiosity" garden includes all the features of an adult garden, including something of interest for every season, it is not a garden that a child could be expected to install. It is intended to fire the imagination of the child, but mom and dad will have to do some of the dirty work.

Start with the structure—the trellis, shrubs and trees—so that the garden has a skeleton to grow on. All of these shrubs and perennials can be planted small, and the plants will grow along with your children. You'll have a landscape that grown-ups can live with in the meantime, too. Plant the perennials and bulbs one section at a time, filling in with annuals—grown from seed, if necessary—to give the garden form and color while it takes shape.

Spider flower

ANNUAL DELIGHTS

Patience is not a virtue of childhood, so be sure to include some annuals in a child's garden. It is possible to substitute annuals for the perennials shown in the accompanying plan, keeping the trees and shrubs for structure and adding bulbs so there will be flowers early in the spring. It may be more fun for children to participate in planting an annual garden, because many of the flowers will come in flats, already in bloom. Unless perennials are purchased in containers of a gallon (3.8l) or more, they will probably not bloom for at least a year. A garden of annuals would probably not be interesting or sophisticated enough to satisfy adult tastes, but kids have no problem with colorful, cheap, and cheerful.

To substitute annuals for perennials in the child's garden, plant one trellis with edible purple hyacinth beans (*Dolichos lablab*, syn. *Dipogon lablab*) and the other with edible scarlet runner beans (*Phaseolus coccineus*)—sow the seeds directly into the soil in late spring. Keep the lamb's ears, the ornamental grass, the wormwood, and the hostas on the plan, because their foliage will look fine the first year. The creeping thyme will also look good from the start, even though it won't be as effective as in later years when it begins to spread. The strawberries, too, will be small but worth keeping.

Mix in exotics with easy-to-find and well-known annuals to keep the curiosity sparked. Plant spider flower (*Cleome hassleriana*) behind the hostas and plant fragrant white flowering tobacco (*Nicotiana alata*) to replace the prairie smoke. Sow seeds of delicate love-in-a-mist (*Nigella damascena*) around the base of the butterfly bush behind the 'Silver Mound'; it will probably reseed for the following year and the seedheads are as interesting as the flowers. Plant tall annual sunflowers in place of the spiky globe thistle, and consider planting a few seeds of dwarf sunflowers in front where kids can meet them eye-to-eye. Another alternative would be to plant the biennial (alternate year flowering and sometimes short-lived) sea holly (*Eryngium giganteum*). It is every bit as spiky and unusual as the perennial in the original plan, and it has the spooky common name of "Miss Willmott's Ghost," after the late British plantswoman Ellen Willmott.

Globe amaranth (*Gomphrena globosa*) is underrated and underused—it flowers so heavily that weeds can't find their way in, thrives even with minimal water and in baking sun, and looks great from early summer until heavy frost. As an added bonus, the flowers are perfect for drying. Try substituting the globe amaranth cultivar 'Lavender Lady' for the perennial gayfeather. Substitute tall, boldly colored zinnias for the bee balm, and plant bushy pure yellow African marigolds (*Tagetes erecta*) in place of the 'Sunray' coreopsis, backed by tall snapdragons or blue salvia such as *Salvia farinacea* 'Victoria'.

Don't forget to include containers in a garden for children—even quirky containers like old red wagons can be drilled for drainage, filled with a good potting soil mixture, and packed with low-growing annuals like impatiens. Another popular theme is a small wooden bed frame filled with a "mattress" of flowers. Topiary, statues, and other gardens ornaments can all find a place in a child's garden. Sure, it can be tacky, but kids *like* tacky.

Underplant annuals with bulbs, just as you would perennials, but use maps or markers to remind you where the bulbs are hiding so you don't disturb them when planting next year's garden. The benefit of an annual garden is that it is relatively inexpensive to plant, especially if some plants are started from seed. The effect is almost instant, and each year the child can choose new flowers and seeds to purchase, sow, and grow. One year the garden might be planted with ornamental fruits, vegetables, and herbs, another year with easy-care shrub roses and fragrant, old-fashioned flowers. There is not as much winter interest as with a perennial garden, but the shrubs and trees do give the garden a skeleton. You can get the best of both worlds by starting the garden with annuals and adding a few more perennials every year, letting the design become more complex and interesting with each year your child—and the garden—grows.

Scarlet runner bean

Children's Curiosity Garden Plant List

1. 'Gracilis' weeping hemlock (*Tsuga canadensis* 'Gracilis')
2. 'Blue Angel' hosta (*Hosta* × 'Blue Angel')
3. 'Alba' cup and saucer flower
     (*Campanula media* var. *calycanthema* 'Alba')
4. 'Horstmann's Silberlocke' Korean fir
     (*Abies koreana* 'Horstmann's Silberlocke')
5. 'Sunray' tickseed (*Coreopsis grandiflora* 'Sunray')
6. Globe thistle (*Echinops ritro*)
7. 'Heavy Metal' switch grass (*Panicum virgatum* 'Heavy Metal')
8. Small-flowered clematis (*Clematis tangutica*)
9. 'Violet Queen' bee balm (*Monarda didyma* 'Violet Queen')
10. 'Black Knight' butterfly bush (*Buddleia davidii* 'Black Knight')
11. 'Silver Mound' wormwood (*Artemisia schmidtiana* 'Silver Mound')
12. 'Pink Panda' strawberry (*Fragaria* × 'Pink Panda')
13. 'Silver Carpet' lamb's ears (*Stachys byzantina* 'Silver Carpet')
14. Passionflower (*Passiflora caerulea*)
15. Globe centaurea (*Centaurea macrocephala*)
16. 'Contorta' Harry Lauder's walking stick
     (*Corylus avellana* 'Contorta')
17. 'Kobold' gayfeather (*Liatris spicata* 'Kobold')
18. Dwarf wild garlic (*Allium karataviense*)
19. Prairie smoke (*Geum triflorum*)
20. 'Grandiflora' PeeGee hydrangea
     (*Hydrangea paniculata* 'Grandiflora')
21. Creeping red thyme (*Thymus serpyllum* var. *coccineus*)
22. 'Diana' rose of Sharon (*Hibiscus siriacus* 'Diana')

Underplant with bulbs to extend your bloom season

'Lutea' yellow crown imperial (*Fritillaria imperialis* 'Lutea')
     —plant in area around cup and saucer plants
'Laverouk' fringed tulip (*Tulipa* × 'Laverouk')
     —plant beneath prairie smoke
'Texas Flame' parrot tulip (*Tulipa* × 'Texas Flame')
     —plant beneath gayfeather
'Praetans Unicum' bouquet tulip (*Tulipa* × 'Praetans Unicum')
     —plant around butterfly bush
Species tulip (*Tulipa tarda*)
     —plant in area around rose of Sharon
'Appeldoorn' Darwin hybrid tulip (*Tulipa* × 'Appeldoorn')
     —plant under globe thistle
'Dutch Master' trumpet daffodil (*Narcissus* × 'Dutch Master')
     —plant under tickseed
'Yellow Mammoth' crocus (*Crocus vernus* 'Yellow Mammoth', syn. 'Dutch Yellow')—plant under and around strawberries
'Golden Splendor' trumpet lily (*Lilium* × 'Golden Splendor')
     —plant behind bee balm

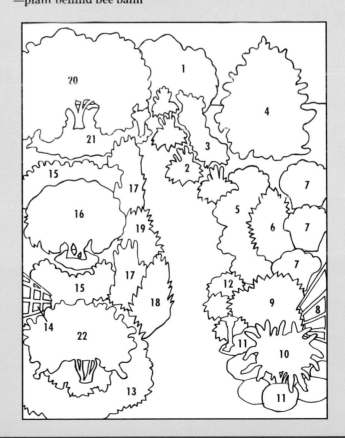

City Courtyard Garden

A limited palette of bronze, purple, green, lavender, and white, along with the neutral colors of slate and brick paving, creates an atmosphere of calm and serenity in this urban courtyard garden. Designed to serve as a personal retreat and as a place to entertain, the garden is constructed on two levels to increase the sense of space and to define areas for dining or even dancing.

Surrounding the upper and lower brick terraces is a densely planted perimeter bed. The rear section of the bed is raised and contained by a stone wall, while the front space is at ground level. In front of the rear wall of the garden, and enclosed by the coping of the raised bed, is a diminutive pond that forms a perfect circle within the rigid lines of the low wall. The pond could be fitted with a small fountain, providing this urban refuge with the soothing splash of falling water—a sound that might mask intrusive city noises.

A pair of exquisite Japanese maples decorates the corners at the back of the garden. While many varieties of Japanese maples would serve this space well, the purple-leafed 'Filiferum Purpureum' is particularly desirable for its strong purple color and lacy leaf. Between the maples, a white wisteria is trained to climb the rear wall or fence—the flush of white flowers gives the

'Deutschland' astilbe

appearance of extended space. In a very long and narrow garden, a purple cultivar would tend to make the area seem a bit shallower.

Two varieties of rhododendrons—the small-leafed 'P.J.M.' and the larger-leafed 'Sappho'—add shape and structure to the upper bed, along with white and lavender-pink flowers in spring. In winter, the 'P.J.M.' rhododendron leaves turn a lovely mahogany-bronze.

Two or three steps join the upper and lower terraces, where a pair of weeping birch trees create a living "wall" separating the upper and lower planting beds. Bunchberry, a low-growing variety of dogwood that is covered with white flowers in late spring and red berries in autumn, makes a dense and attractive groundcover in the lower bed while massive blue-green 'Elegans' hostas carpet the upper bed. 'Purple Palace' coral bells, with their bronze-purple leaves and white flowers, white astilbe, and white clematis complete this scheme.

You may wish to alter some of the elements in this plan to better suit your existing courtyard space. The plants in the plan will work equally well with any number of alterations to the hardscape. Once the plants are in place, this garden is exceedingly low maintenance, and will look good year after year.

Keeping Your Plants in Bounds

A courtyard garden, by its very nature, is a garden where space is limited. In a courtyard, plants that become too large can't be moved to a more appropriate spot elsewhere on the property. Select only plants that will confine their growth to the space allocated to them or those that can be successfully pruned.

For some reason, gardeners are often terrified by the idea of pruning. Though an important task and one that requires some skill, it is hardly difficult to master. In this garden design, there is only a bit of routine pruning. Japanese maples are very slow-growing trees and should require little or no pruning with the exception of removing the occasional dead twig. Wisteria, an aggressive grower, will bloom more profusely when it has been heavily pruned. As you pick up your pruners, follow these simple rules.

1. Using the right tools is essential to a successful pruning job. Small hand pruners are required for most pruning, but you may need larger loppers if pruning needs have been ignored for some time or if there has been considerable damage to tree limbs from disease or injury. Before you make the first cut, have the pruner blades professionally sharpened.

2. Many flowering shrubs should be pruned after they have flowered. Cut the branches that bloomed down to the base in order to allow for new growth. The flower buds will appear on this new wood the following year.

3. Broad-leaved evergreen flowering shrubs generally need only to have their spent flowers removed. If these shrubs should begin to outgrow their spaces, prune them back at a node (the small swelling on a branch or stem from which a bud or leaf grows).

4. Pruning cuts should be made on a sharp angle, with the cut angling away from the plant. This allows water to run off rather than collect, which could cause rot.

5. A word of caution: few trees or shrubs will react well to being topped, that is, having the leader or primary vertical stems cut off. To avoid having to top a tree, study the growth habits of trees you are considering for your courtyard garden and only select those varieties that will not grow too tall for the site. If you "inherit" a tree in your courtyard that has become too tall, engage the services of a licensed arborist to do the heavy pruning. Allow the tree to be topped only if there is no other solution.

Japanese wisteria

'P. J. M.' rhododendron

CITY COURTYARD GARDEN PLANT LIST

1. 'Issai Perfect' wisteria (*Wisteria* 'Issai Perfect')
2. 'Elegans' hosta (*Hosta sieboldiana* 'Elegans')
3. 'Deutschland' astilbe (*Astilbe* 'Deutschland')
4. 'Filiferum Purpureum' laceleaf Japanese maple
    (*Acer palmatum* 'Filiferum Purpureum')
5. 'P.J.M.' rhododendron (*Rhododendron* 'P.J.M.')
6. 'Sappho' rhododendron (*Rhododendron* 'Sappho')
7. Weeping birch (*Betula pendula*)
8. 'Purple Palace' coral bells (*Heuchera micrantha* 'Purple Palace')
9. Henry clematis (*Clematis hernryii*)
10. Bunchberry (*Cornus canadensis*)

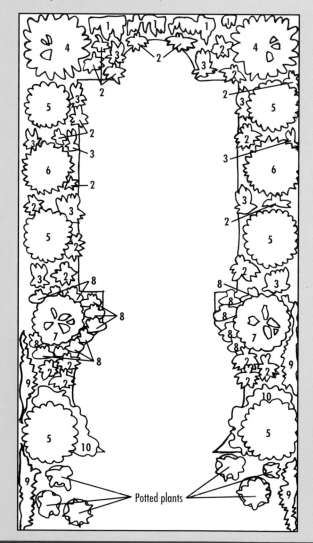

Potted plants

Container Garden

Wooden decks have become wildly popular in recent years. Regardless of climate or building style or the age and history of the surrounding neighborhood, these open-air porches have proliferated. If well-designed and soundly constructed, decks can be an ideal means of integrating your home with your garden. Sometimes, though, they are nearly uninhabitable during hot summer days, since they have often been built without any consideration for the value of cooling shade.

This garden design solves the problem of shade, and creates a space that is both pleasing to look at and easy to live in. Beautiful as well as practical, a wooden pergola covers the area just outside the back door to provide some needed relief from the summer sun. A trellis along one side of the pergola gives support to a grape vine, which will eventually canopy the area and create a sense of privacy. The woodwork is open enough so as to not seriously restrict the light coming into the house in the winter and spring, but in the summer the lush foliage of the grape vine ensures a relatively cool and comfortable refuge. In autumn, the spectacular color of the grape leaves will enliven the entire scene. Benches are built in along the sides of the deck, both in sun and shade. This is an exceedingly practical way to provide seating because the benches can also open up to store gardening equipment.

Even an architecturally flawless deck may seem barren and incomplete if not accompanied by a skillfully designed and executed planting plan. A deck is a perfect opportunity to grow a great diversity of plants in different kinds of containers; it is one of the few situations where one specimen of a plant may well be ideal, where the design dictate to plant in drifts may be comfortably ignored. Container gardening offers a chance to experiment, to try all sorts of plants that you might otherwise be too timid to use. Place them in bold combinations, and if you don't like the way they look or they don't thrive in their situation, you can simply move them.

A garden on a deck provides the perfect place for the lush blooms and prominent leaves of tropical plants like angel's trumpet. Set this lovely flower out once the weather is warm, and you'll evoke the sultry exuberance of the tropics without looking unnatural or contrived. Here is an opportunity, moreover, to be artistically daring with no great risk because design or cultural mistakes can be easily rectified.

This is not to suggest, however, that annuals are the only plants suitable for containers. If this were the case, the garden

Scented geranium

would be a sad wasteland in winter and early spring. Even in a garden made up exclusively of containers, it is important to include plants that will provide consistent form and structure. These plants will anchor the garden and ensure that it remains interesting long after the annuals have either succumbed to frost or been brought inside for the winter. In this design, annuals are accompanied by two root-hardy conifers—boulevard false cypress and an upright juniper cultivar called 'Moonglow'—as well as by heavenly bamboo, an evergreen shrub that is loveliest in the autumn and winter. The deciduous shrubs hydrangea and butterfly bush, along with a selection of ornamental grasses, also provide lasting interest. The grasses—feather reed grass (a small cultivar of fountain grass) and the more tender lemon grass—are as beautiful in winter, though in a different way, as they are in summer and autumn.

Other herbaceous perennials are also included, notably Siberian iris, a dense, icy blue stonecrop, Russian sage, daylilies, thyme, and three water-loving plants (water lily, variegated sweet flag, and rush). More on the marginal side of hardiness are the various salvias, lily of the Nile, and rosemary; if the winter is not too cold and icy and the plants are well-drained, they may well survive.

Since many of the perennials do not look like much until late spring and the annuals can be set out only once there is no longer a risk of frost, early-blooming bulbs are essential. Bulbs will manage fine in containers as long as they have excellent drainage through the winter. You can facilitate this by placing a layer of small pottery shards or gravel at the bottom of the container before adding soil. Daffodils, tulips, hyacinths, and Dutch irises bloom in the sunny part of the garden and can in fact be combined in a small area by layering them. The shaded area under the pergola is illuminated in spring by the pale blue and white blossoms of Spanish bluebells.

Angel's trumpet

Underplanting trees, shrubs, and large perennials grown in containers will give the garden a more finished, refined look. Assuming the primary plant will not shade out the underplanting, this second layer will also make the pot more interesting over a longer period of time. In this design the Russian sage grown in a pot is accompanied by silver thyme and *Salvia chamaedryoides*, echoing the table planting nearby. The steel blue foliage of *Juniperus scopularum* 'Moonglow', for another example, is echoed and intensified by the icy blue leaves of the *Sedum dasyphyllum* planted underneath. An alternative to underplanting every pot is to top dress some containers with small river stones. These stones are colorful and elegant, and will help preserve moisture and suppress weeds. When the river stones are wet from the rain they are truly glorious.

Many plants are well suited to life in a container.

CARING FOR PLANTS IN CONTAINERS

Good hygiene will minimize future problems with your plants; the best way to begin is with clean pots and sterile soil. Porous containers like terra-cotta and stone should be cleaned especially well and should be moistened before planting. Layer small pottery shards or gravel in the bottom of the container to facilitate drainage. In a large pot this layer should be several inches thick. The potting soil you use is largely a matter of taste, but also depends on the type of plant being grown, the kind of container you plan to use, and how much you wish to spend. The simplest alternative is to buy a commercial potting soil. Peat-based potting soils tend to dry out quite quickly, while soil-based ones are heavier and can become compacted. The best solution may be to mix the two kinds of commercial products so your soil is neither too heavy nor too light. If your prepared soil does not already contain perlite, it is advantageous to add some; the perlite has no nutritional value but it does improve the aeration and water retention of the soil.

Plants grown in containers undoubtedly have a tendency to dry out quicker than those grown in the ground. This can lead to wilted, stunted growth and a general failure to thrive. Sometimes we overcompensate, however, and water pots and hanging baskets to the point that they become waterlogged, causing root rot and other problems. Again, the best solution is a careful balance—don't let your containers dry out completely but be careful not to overwater. How often you need to water will of course depend in part on the specific moisture requirements of the plants you are growing. In this design, the hydrangea, angel's trumpet, lily of the Nile, and Siberian irises all demand a great deal of moisture and will very much resent being thirsty. The herbs, grasses, and juniper, on the other hand, are quite drought-tolerant, and may be watered less often.

Consider also the location of your pots. Plants positioned in full sun will obviously lose moisture more quickly than those in the shade, as will plants sited in the path of drying winds. Moisture-loving plants will certainly perform better if kept in a location somewhat sheltered from the wind. Check your containers daily, even in rainy weather, to ensure that they are getting the correct amount of water.

We expect a lot from container plants, especially annuals. We want them to grow large and lush and bloom profusely, often in a fairly short period of time. To ensure that they meet our expectations, a regular feeding program is advisable, especially for notoriously heavy feeders like angel's trumpet, lily of the Nile, and fuchsia. These plants, along with the hanging baskets, will flower best if fed weekly during the growing season with a water-soluble fertilizer. The herbs and grasses do not require such attention, and will in fact perform poorly in overly fertile soil. They do not need or want supplemental feeding and if they are doing poorly it is more likely because of inadequate light or poor drainage. The other herbaceous plants, including the water lilies, fall somewhere in between these two extremes and will appreciate being fertilized every two to four weeks, though feeding should stop around midsummer to avoid promoting a great flush of tender new growth too late in the growing season.

Plants kept alive in a container year after year will certainly become pot-bound over time. This means that the roots of the plant, having spread as far as they can in the pot, will start to wrap around and around the root ball. This will eventually kill the plant if it is not removed from the pot it has outgrown and transferred to a slightly larger one. Before repotting it is critical to loosen the bound roots and to gently pry them apart and prune them back a bit so they will be able to grow unobstructed once set in the larger container.

How often a plant will need to be repotted will, of course, depend upon the specific plant and how fast it grows, as well as on the size of the pot in which it starts

out. At least once a year check the perennials, shrubs, and trees that you have growing in pots by tilting the pot sideways and carefully examining the root ball. Do not wait until a problem develops, for root pruning and repotting can be done whenever the plant is growing and is almost always beneficial.

The plants you leave out in pots during the winter (other than the annuals that you simply forgot about; they are most likely dead) will, in most cases, be dormant until the weather warms up in the spring. The best way to help them survive their winter dormancy is to make sure that they are very well watered through the autumn, before they stop growing. It is also critical that they remain well drained and that water does not sit on the plants, relentlessly freezing and thawing and almost certainly causing them to eventually heave out of the soil. Evergreen boughs will provide some protection, though a persistent snow cover is even better.

In a relatively temperate climate you can continue to water your pots regularly. They obviously will not require as much water as when they are vigorously growing. Conifers in pots are very susceptible to drying out in winter, especially if they are located in a windswept site. Check their soil often and water as needed, though never when temperatures are at or close to freezing. When choosing your containers, remember that terra-cotta pots will crack if left outside in very cold weather. If you plan to leave your pots outside in a cold climate consider using faux terra-cotta (which is usually made of metal, plastic, or some composite material), wood, concrete, or some other material that can survive the temperature extremes unscathed.

The water plants in the little tub in this design are not particularly tender, but because the pool is so small it is likely to freeze if left outside through the winter. It is probably safest to bring the table and plants inside to a sunny room until the weather is warmer or let them go semi-dormant in a relatively cool area like your garage. This table should be at least six inches (15cm) deep to accommodate the roots of the water lilies.

CONTAINER GARDEN PLANT LIST

1. Grape vine (*Vitis amurensis*)
2. 'Caesar's Brother' Siberian iris (*Iris sibirica* 'Caesar's Brother')
3. 'Diadem' hydrangea (*Hydrangea serrata* 'Diadem')
4. Ferns on potting table:
   a. 'Rochfordianum' Japanese holly fern (*Cyrtomium falcatum* 'Rochfordianum')
   b. Shaggy shield fern (*Dryopteris atrata*)
   c. Oriental fern (*Athyrium vidalii*)
   d. Auriculate lady fern (*Athyrium otophorum*)
5. 'Moyer's Red' heavenly bamboo (*Nandina domestica* 'Moyer's Red')
6. 'Karl Foerster' feather reed grass (*Calamagrostis* × *acutiflora* 'Karl Foerster')
7. 'Headbourne Bressingham Blue' lily of the Nile (*Agapanthus* 'Headbourne Bressingham Blue')
8. 'Alabama Crimson' honeysuckle (*Lonicera sempervirens* 'Alabama Crimson')
9. Hanging baskets:
   a. 'Barbara Tingley' ornamental oregano (*Origanum* × 'Barbara Tingley')
   b. Bellflower (*Campanula hawkinsiana*)
   c. 'Palace Passion' coralbells (*Heuchera* 'Palace Passion')
   d. Winged pea (*Lotus berthelotii*)
   e. Spreading zinnia (*Zinnia angustifolia*)
10. 'Riffense' stonecrop (*Sedum dasyphyllum* 'Riffense')
11. Scented geraniums:
    a. Attar of roses (*Pelargonium graveolens*)
    b. Ginger (*Pelargonium* 'Torento')
    c. 'Mrs. Taylor' (*Pelargonium ignescens* 'Mrs. Taylor')
12. 'Filagran' Russian sage (*Perovskia atriplicifolia* 'Filagran')—underplant with silver thyme (*Thymus* 'Argenteus') and sage (*Salvia chamaedryoides*)
13. Angel's trumpet (*Brugmansia versicolor*)
14. 'Grosso' fat spike lavender (*Lavandula intermedia* 'Grosso')
15. 'Ruby Throat' daylily (*Hemerocallis* 'Ruby Throat')
16. 'Cassian' fountain grass (*Pennisetum alopecuroides* 'Cassian')
17. 'Moonglow' upright juniper (*Juniperus scopulorum* 'Moonglow')—underplant with 'Riffense' stonecrop (*Sedum dasyphyllum* 'Riffense')
18. Large table:
    a. Silver thyme (*Thymus* 'Argenteus')
    b. Sage (*Salvia chamaedryoides*)
    c. 'Desert Blaze' sage (*Salvia greggii* 'Desert Blaze')

19. 'Nanho Blue' butterfly bush (*Buddleia davidii* 'Nanho Blue')—underplant with 'Barbara Tingley' oregano (*Origanum* × 'Barbara Tingley'), spreading zinnia (*Zinnia angustifolia*), and sage (*Salvia chamaedryoides*)
20. Boulevard false cypress (*Chamaecyparis pisifera* 'Boulevard')
21. Lemongrass (*Cymbopogon citratus*)
22. 'Arp' rosemary (*Rosmarinus officinalis* 'Arp')
23. 'Woodside Fire Dance' daylily (*Hemerocallis* 'Woodside Fire Dance')
24. Pond table:
    a. 'Walter Pagels' water lily (*Nymphaea* 'Walter Pagels')
    b. 'Variegatus' sweet flag (*Acorus gramineus* 'Variegatus')
    c. Rush (*Juncus glaucus*)

YOU MAY ALSO WISH TO INCLUDE SOME SPRING-FLOWERING BULBS TO EXTEND THE BLOOM SEASON

'Jenny' daffodil (*Narcissus* 'Jenny')
'Buffawn' daffodil (*Narcissus* 'Buffawn')
'Tangerine Beauty' tulip (*Tulipa vedenskyi* 'Tangerine Beauty')
'Borah' hyacinth (*Hyacinthus* 'Borah')
'Edward' Dutch iris (*Iris reticulata* 'Edward')
'Blue Queen' Spanish bluebells (*Hyacinthoides hispanica* 'Blue Queen')

Four Seasons Garden

For many years, gardening was considered a summer pastime, with a slight overlapping of seasons in spring and autumn. Bedding plants filled window boxes, lined walks, spilled out of containers, and paraded like stiff little colorful soldiers up and down the sides of driveways. Adventurous souls cut circular or oval island beds into the center of the lawn and displayed riotous beds of annuals, changing the theme and color schemes of these beds every year. The wealthy had conservatories, solariums, greenhouses, or lean-to shelters that helped bring the garden indoors for the winter. Green was provided by yew, juniper, pine, and spruce but, apart from garden structures and statuary, winter gardens for the most part were ghostly spaces shrouded in white. Luckily, times have changed.

While annual gardens generally bloom from planting until frost, novice gardeners are often daunted by the trick of planting perennials that will not only complement each other, but that will also bloom together. It is easy to find photographs in garden books of massive perennial beds with virtually everything in bloom at the same time. This might look impressive at the time, but what will those gardens look like for the rest of the season? Annuals, shrub roses, and long-blooming perennials can stretch from sea-

Periwinkle

son to season but where, apart from Florida, do you find plants in bloom in every month? The answer is, of course, that you don't. A four seasons garden is most likely to reflect the climatic vagaries of each region, so don't be afraid to make substitutions if a particular plant is known to be problematic in your area.

This garden plan features a Japanese black pine instead of a white (*P. strobus*), Austrian (*P. nigra*), or Scotch pine (*P. sylvestris*) because the latter three have been so over-planted that they are now being ravaged by pests and diseases. Also, the white "candles" of Japanese black pine are so striking against its dark green needles. The coral bark maple provides bright winter branches, while the prolific red fruits of the winterberry will bring bright color and attract wildlife to the garden. The compact American cranberrybush viburnum has attractive creamy white flowers in late spring to early summer, followed by handsome three-cornered leaves and finally brilliant autumn color. The 'Donald Wyman' crab apple looks great all year—named after the Arnold Arboretum's late, great plantsman and author, this crab apple is fairly broad and upright when young but is wide and spreading at maturity. This lovely tree flowers prolifically in spring and bears small, persistent red fruits.

Leave the ornamental grasses as they are at the end of the season—they don't even have to be pruned in spring, though many will benefit if you choose to cut them back. The hostas will wither away after a few frosts; pull out the flower stalks once the foliage has dried up. Many of the perennials included in this plan put on a show that lasts all summer, although a large part of the garden will be at its best in late summer and early autumn. By underplanting the garden with bulbs, spring can be equally colorful. Removing spent flowers on the perennials will encourage many of them to a second, if less consistent, period of bloom. While all new plants need a regular program of watering until they become established, once it is established this garden should require minimal watering. All of the plants shown are relatively hardy, disease resistant, and require little pruning or other special maintenance. Apart from a little deadheading and watering, about three applications of fertilizer in early summer, and cutting back dead foliage in early spring, the plants featured in this design should give you several seasons of enjoyment for a relatively small investment of time and labor.

A Winter Wonderland

A four seasons garden puts more of an emphasis on winter than most garden designs, even though it is not just a winter garden. Snow acts as a wonderful insulator to protect plants from drying winter winds, but it may also cause problems in four season gardens. For example, it is difficult to admire small winter aconites, miniscule snowdrops, and even crocuses when they are covered in snow. If that was all the snow covered, it wouldn't be so bad, but in many areas it is not all that unusual to have a fairly substantial snow cover even at the end of April. A heavy, wet snow will break branches on conifers, bend ornamental grasses in half, and entirely cover low-growing conifers, shrubs, and early-flowering perennials such as hellebores. Once they have been squashed by snow, sleds, and the booted feet of children, the ornamental value of many small plants has been destroyed.

Luckily, this type of winter damage does not happen every day, even in cold climates. When it does, though, you can minimize the damage by using a broom to carefully knock heavy snow off of your conifers, birches, ornamental grasses, and small, fragile shrubs. Gardeners in areas that are prone to deep snow cover may want to place more focus on taller garden elements for winter interest, selecting plants that will still be visible no matter how deep the snow drifts or how long it holds on.

Snowdrops

Yellow and red twig dogwoods form dense thickets (their color is best when they are regularly pruned and thinned) that can take the cold, and they can be pruned to just about any height. The green branches of *Kerria japonica* 'Pleniflora', the silvery-purple arching branches of wild blackberries (very invasive but beautiful in winter), and the unusual bark patterns of sycamore (*Platanus occidentalis*), lacebark pine (*Pinus bungeana*), river birch (*Betula nigra*), striped maple (*Acer pensylvanicum*), and amur cherry (*Prunus maackii*) will rise above just about any snowdrifts. Beware of planting early-flowering trees like magnolia in areas where sudden frosts can strike even in late spring—the flower buds will die before they've ever had a chance to bloom. Try witch hazel (*Hamamelis* × 'Arnold's Promise') instead—its spidery flowers are not showy but they are among the first to appear, often shortly before the forsythia blooms.

One more word of advice for gardeners in cold regions—plant lots of the tallest, goldest daffodils you can find, along with early-flowering peonies and tulips. By the time the late-flowering varieties bloom the lilacs and crab apples will be stealing the show, but those first flowers in spring will steal your heart.

Four Seasons Garden Plant List

1. 'Winter Red' winterberry (*Ilex verticillata* 'Winter Red')
2. 'Frances Williams' hosta (*Hosta* × 'Frances Williams')
3. 'Luxuriant' bleeding heart (*Dicentra eximia* 'Luxuriant')
4. 'Bright Star' purple coneflower (*Echinacea purpurea* 'Bright Star')
5. 'Thunderhead' Japanese black pine (*Pinus thunbergii* 'Thunderhead')
6. Russian sage (*Perovskia atriplicifolia*)
7. 'Blue' balloon flower (*Platycodon grandiflora* 'Blue')
8. 'Sangu Kaku' coral bark maple (*Acer palmatum* 'Sangu Kaku', syn. 'Senkaki')
9. Purple Japanese silver grass (*Miscanthus sinensis* var. *purpurascens*)
10. 'Autumn Joy' showy stonecrop (*Hylotelephium telephium* 'Autumn Joy', formerly listed as a cross of *Sedum spectabile* and *Sedum telephium*)
11. 'Goldsturm' orange coneflower (*Rudbeckia fulgida* 'Goldsturm', syn. 'Goldsturm Strain')
12. Paperbark maple (*Acer griseum*)
13. 'Stella d'Oro' compact daylily (*Hemerocallis* × 'Stella d'Oro')
14. 'Little Bunny' dwarf fountain grass (*Pennisetum alopecurides* 'Little Bunny')
15. 'Compacta' American cranberrybush viburnum (*Viburnum trilobum* 'Compacta')
16. 'Snowstorm' coral bells (*Heuchera sanguinea* 'Snowstorm')
17. 'Donald Wyman' crab apple (*Malus* × 'Donald Wyman')
18. 'Coral 'n' Gold' peony (*Paeonia* × 'Coral 'n' Gold'), at base of crab apple, inside tree circle
19. 'Sterling Silver' perennial periwinkle (*Vinca minor* 'Sterling Silver')

Underplant with Bulbs to Extend the Bloom Season in Your Garden

'Cream Beauty' crocus (*Crocus* × 'Cream Beauty')—plant some around the base of each tree

'Daydream' trumpet daffodils (*Narcissus* × 'Daydream')—plant under hostas

'Apricot Beauty' tulips (*Tulipa* × 'Apricot Beauty')—plant under coral bells

'Queen of the Night' tulips (*Tulipa* × 'Queen of the Night')—plant under purple coneflowers

'Shirley' tulips (*Tulipa* × 'Shirley')—plant under balloon flowers

'Arabian Mystery' tulips (*Tulipa* × 'Arabian Mystery')—plant under bleeding heart

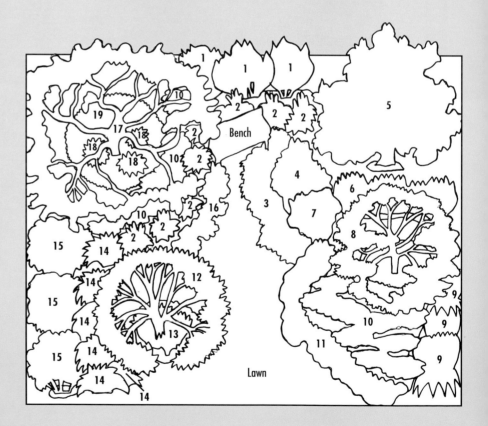

Fragrant Garden

A garden without fragrance seems somehow one-dimensional. What a disappointment to lean into the face of a beautiful rose only to inhale—and smell nothing. In the same way that smelling salts can jolt someone into consciousness, the scent of a garden can stir the blood and awaken memories long forgotten. Scent is a very personal thing, and many people have strong feelings about the fragrance of different plants. What is ambrosia to one person may be abhorrent to another.

Fragrance is often fleeting—how often have you stood in a garden, sniffing the air and trying to pinpoint the source of something wonderful that teased your senses? One plant's fragrance might be the slightest suggestion carried on a breeze, while another's might be overpowering and almost too sweet. The scent of certain plants becomes more pronounced after dark, while other plants need to be brushed, touched, or crushed in order to release their fragrance. In some plants the fragrance is in the flowers; in other plants, it's the foliage that bears the scent.

The fragrant garden featured here will peak in spring and early summer, with a few plants holding their own until autumn. Although each plant is considered fragrant, they will not all release their perfume at the same time of day or at the same point during the season. The scent of some perennials and shrubs, if they are planted when they are small, may not become apparent until the plants have had time to become established. The bulbs and roses will bloom the first year, though, as should most of the shrubs. 'Sir Thomas Lipton' is a fairly hardy rugosa rose while 'William Shakespeare' is one of the new English roses—neither should require exceptional care. Lily-of-the-valley smells so good it has to be included in a fragrance garden, but it is tricky to situate; it should be confined by a path, wall, or tree circle to control its tendency toward rapid spreading.

Train vines such as 'Odorata' anemone clematis against the deck or wall, and in a few years the fragrance will be everywhere. Tender plants such as Chilean jasmine can be treated as annuals—plant them in containers and then train them against the deck or a trellis. Other tender, strongly fragrant bulbs such as tuberose (*Polianthes tuberosa* 'The Pearl') and the spider lily (*Hymenocallis × festalis*, sometimes called *Ismene festalis*) can be planted in containers in cold regions and over-wintered in a sheltered spot such as a garage. Underplant hostas with 'Regale' lilies—after their wonderful fragrance fades and the trumpet-shaped flowers wither away, the foliage of the hostas will disguise the lilies' spindly stalks.

Lily-of-the-Valley

It is fairly simple to extend the garden season by planting in layers—planting early- and late-blooming bulbs beneath perennials will give you a longer season of bloom. The bulbs of lilies, daffodils, and hyacinths are usually planted deep enough that they don't interfere with the roots of perennials, while the tiny bulbs of grape hyacinth, crocus, glory-of-the-snow, and windflowers can be scattered around the perennials by digging them in at relatively shallow depths. Dig in some bone meal or "bulb booster" fertilizer at the time of planting, too. Bulbs almost always look better planted in large masses, and some will cooperate by naturalizing and spreading. Tulip and hyacinth bulbs are a little fussy, and will probably have to be replaced after a few years. Remember that bigger is not always better—while the large blossoms of trumpet daffodils and Darwin tulips are certainly showy, the smaller daffodils of the *Narcissus triandrus*, *N. cyclamineus*, *N. tazetta*, and *N. poeticus* types, as well as the small species tulips, can be equally effective when planted in large groups. All of the bulbs featured are very fragrant, although sometimes the scent is more noticeable when the flowers are cut and brought into a warm house.

Finally, don't just look to flowers for fragrance—some of the most fragrant plants are shrubs, trees, or herbs. There is a reason why manufacturers of cleaning supplies imitate the scent of pine, why incense burners are sold with fragrant blocks of balsam fir—even common junipers can smell wonderful. Fill your garden with all types of fragrance, then sit outside, close your eyes—and inhale.

PARSLEY, SAGE, ROSEMARY, AND THYME

Many herbs are aromatic, even pungent, and they can be used both as culinary accents and as ornamentals in the garden. Most herbs require at least half a day of sun, so the best place for herbs in this fragrant garden plan would be in containers on the deck, where they can be moved to catch the most sun. If the deck is handy to the kitchen, the cook may find the portable herb garden ideal for obtaining a pinch of basil, a touch of tarragon, or an ounce of oregano. Herbs seem to be made for handling—rub a basil leaf and then smell your fingers. Plant lavender or thyme between paving stones or at the edges of a path so their fragrance will be released when brushed or stepped on.

Scented geraniums are available in almost every fragrance under the sun: attar of rose, nutmeg, cinnamon rose, lemon rose, mint, ginger, orange, coconut, lime, apple, apricot, strawberry, and more. All can be grown in containers and brought indoors over the winter; some have culinary uses, others are ideal in hanging baskets or as bedding plants. A few, such as fern leaf, strawberry, ginger, and 'Mabel Grey' scented geraniums can be used for topiary. Lime, nutmeg, southernwood, and 'French Lace' scented geraniums can even be pruned into bonsai forms.

Mint is one of the most fragrant herbs, and also one of the most prolific. Many gardeners, when planting it in a bed, first place it in a metal coffee container and then bury the container. If you want to keep this invasive plant from spreading, don't trust even that method, and confine it to containers resting on concrete. Despite its tendency to spread, mint is a must for a fragrant herb garden. Spearmint, peppermint, applemint, English applemint, pineapple mint, orange mint, chocolate mint, variegated Scotch mint, Corsican mint (a tender groundcover for moist shade), wild horsemint, wild native mint, and English pennyroyal (similar to citronella) are all extremely fragrant. Spearmint, applemint, and English applemint are the best choices for culinary use; peppermint and orange mint make the best teas.

Half the fun of growing herbs is smelling them, and there are scores of ways to add herbs to your fragrant garden. Fill containers, strawberry pots, and even hanging baskets with fragrant herbs and position them where you can see and smell them. Soon you will be making a place for herbs in the house and in the perennial border. Next you'll find yourself cutting and drying herbs for cooking and crafts, and before long, your house and garden are sure to be overflowing with a potpourri of fragrant herbs.

FRAGRANT GARDEN PLANT LIST

1. 'Mohawk' viburnum (*Viburnum × burkwoodii* 'Mohawk')
2. 'Royal Star' magnolia (*Magnolia stellata* 'Royal Star')
3. 'Zing Rose' maiden pinks (*Dianthus deltoides* 'Zing Rose')
4. Variegated Solomon's seal (*Polygonatum odoratum* 'Variegatum')
5. 'Festiva Maxima' peony (*Paeonia × 'Festiva Maxima'*)
6. 'Sir Thomas Lipton' rose (*Rosa rugosa* 'Sir Thomas Lipton')
7. 'David' phlox (*Phlox paniculata* 'David')
8. 'William Shakespeare' English rose (*Rosa × 'William Shakespeare'*)
9. Sweet woodruff (*Asperula odorata*)
10. 'Miss Ellen Willmott' common lilac (*Syringa vulgaris* 'Miss Ellen Willmott')
11. Lily-of-the-valley (*Convallaria majalis*)
12. 'Odorata' anemone clematis (*Clematis montana* var. *rubens* 'Odorata') (space at intervals to train along sides of deck)
13. Chilean jasmine (*Mandevilla laxa*) (in container on deck)
14. 'Superba' littleleaf lilac (*Syringa microphylla* 'Superba')
15. 'Fragrant Blue' hosta (*Hosta × 'Fragrant Blue'*)
16. 'Hummingbird' dwarf summersweet (*Clethra alnifolia* 'Hummingbird')
17. 'Royal Standard' hosta (*Hosta × 'Royal Standard'*)
18. Koreanspice viburnum (*Viburnum carlesii*)
19. 'White Czar' white violet (*Viola odorata* 'White Czar')

BULBS FOR UNDERPLANTING

White trumpet lily (*Lilium regale* 'Album')—plant beneath 'Royal Standard' hostas

'Cheerfulness' daffodil (*Narcissus × 'Cheerfulness'*)—plant beneath 'Fragrant Blue' hostas

'Winston Churchill' daffodil (*Narcissus × 'Winston Churchill'*)—plant around base of Koreanspice viburnum, along with 'Trevithian' daffodils

'Erlicheer' daffodil (*Narcissus × 'Erlicheer'*)—plant around base of star magnolia, along with hyacinths

'Actea' daffodil (*Narcissus × 'Actea'*)— plant beneath 'David' phlox, along with 'Sinopel' daffodil

'Sinopel' daffodil (*Narcissus × 'Sinopel'*) —plant beneath 'David' phlox, along with 'Actea' daffodil

'Trevithian' daffodil (*Narcissus × 'Trevithian'*)—plant around base of Koreanspice viburnum, along with 'Sir Winston Churchill' daffodil

'Geranium' daffodil (*Narcissus × 'Geranium'*)—plant beneath Solomon's seal along walk

'Crystal Palace' hyacinth (*Hyacinthus × 'Crystal Palace'*)—plant around base of star magnolia with 'Erlicheer' daffodil; also plant in front of peonies

Moonlight Garden

Moonlight becomes you. . ." So goes an old song, but in truth, moonlight becomes just about anything. There's a reason for all those "moon" and "June" verses and lyrics—the dark of a summer evening, lit only by the moon, can be equally redolent of memories and mystery, magic and romance. The summer sun can be harsh, but the thought of walking through a moonlit garden on a warm summer's evening—teased by soft fragrances carried on a breeze or released by brushing your hand against a leaf— brings a feeling of serenity.

One evening as the sun begins to set, take note of the changes in your garden as the dimming light casts shadows and takes away the colors of the flowers. Long after the red flowers have paled to gray, the white flowers glimmer and sometimes glow in the falling darkness—especially when the moon is full. Tennyson described it more poetically: "Now sleeps the crimson, now the white. . ." Some flowers curl into themselves in the heat of day, only opening after sundown. Especially magical are those flowers whose fragrance intensifies in the cool darkness of evening— although relatively few flowers actually release their fragrance after dark.

There is not much point in having a "moonlight garden" if you never spend time in your garden after dark. Likewise, a fragrant evening garden serves no purpose if it will only be observed through a window. For this reason, the accompanying plan is set around a deck (a patio would work as well)—add a few close friends, comfortable lounge chairs, a few strategically placed citronella torches, and a couple of tall glasses of iced tea and you will be well placed to relax and enjoy this mostly fragrant moonlight garden. If your deck or patio is laid out differently or if it only allows for a garden on one side, simply eliminate the duplicate half of the garden. If you don't have a deck or a patio, shift the direction of the plan so that it can be adapted to fit your front porch or the area under your kitchen window.

Regal trumpet lily

Most people think of a moonlight garden as an all-white garden, but white is not the only color that glows in the dark. In my garden, I have noticed that *Scabiosa* × 'Butterfly Blue' starts to sizzle as the dusk diffuses the colors of other plants around it, giving it a purpley glow that reminds me of a black light's luminescence. The lavender flowers of hostas sometimes show a similar effect. At the same time, the white flowers of some plants seem too matte to reflect the moonlight, and just look drab and pale. Most blues and reds blend into the night, but sometimes a yellow flower will "reach out in the darkness." Experiment with light-colored foliage plants, with white-flowering shrubs, and with white-flowering annuals and bulbs to extend the season. Public gardens and arboreta aren't usually open to visitors after dusk, so you may have to visit the gardens of your friends at night to get new ideas for your moonlight garden.

Don't rely on books to tell you which plants are best for fragrance—fragrance is too arbitrary and personal. In the first place, not everyone can detect the more subtle scents, and not everyone likes the stronger ones. I love the scents of mock orange and of lilac, but I know others who loathe their perfume. And while some plants have a stronger fragrance in the evening, others seem to radiate perfume in the heat of day. Other people can offer suggestions, but perhaps more than any other type of garden, a fragrant moonlight garden needs the tender touch—and sensitive nose—of its own caretaker.

Because a moonlight garden needs to be enjoyed from the outside of the house, this garden will reach its peak during the warmth of summer. If your region enjoys mild springs, extend the usefulness of the moonlight garden by adding fragrant daffodils, hyacinths, fragrant white peonies, and white-flowering spring shrubs. There are many white-flowering perennials that can extend the garden into the autumn, but for the most part, these late bloomers are not fragrant.

Although it is not always necessary, deadheading (removing spent flowers) will often

The problem with some flowers is not that they aren't wonderful, night-flowering, and/or night-fragrant—the problem is availability. Talk to other gardeners, look in plant books, reference books, design books, and you will come up with a very long list of recommended plants. When it comes to finding a source for these plants, it's another story. Botanical names change and change again, flowers gain popularity only to fade into obscurity—pinning down the flowers you want can turn into a treasure hunt or maybe a wild goose chase.

In his 1953 book *Fragrance in the Garden*, Norman Taylor describes the "night witchery" of certain plants, and recommends his favorites. Thousands more flowers are in production now than there were in 1953, but Taylor's choices are still hard to find: night phlox (*Zaluzianskya villosa*), jasmine tobacco (*Nicotiana alata* 'Grandiflora'), evening campion (*Lychnis alba*), a night-flowering annual from Chile (*Schizopetalon walkeri*), a wild species of gladiolus (*Gladiolus tristis*), a Japanese daylily (*Hemerocallis thunbergii*), and the tufted evening primrose (*Oenothera caespitosa*). If you should come across any of these, be sure to give it a prized place in your moonlight garden

Flowering tobacco

encourage another flush of bloom. Once the plants have become established, there will be plenty of flowers to cut so you can bring the fragrance into your house. In well-drained soil, rich in organic matter, the lilies will flourish and multiply. The flowering tobacco, sweet rocket, and night-flowering stock may not survive the winter in all areas but all the other plants listed are extremely hardy. The rugosa rose 'Blanc Double de Coubert' is one of the hardiest old roses—cover the canes with a loose pile of shredded leaves over the winter (no styrofoam cones!), removing them in early spring.

'The Pearl' sneezewort

MOONLIGHT GARDEN PLANT LIST

1. Koreanspice viburnum (*Viburnum carlesii*)
2. 'Miss Ellen Willmott' white lilac (*Syringa vulgaris* 'Miss Ellen Willmott')
3. 'The Pearl' sneezewort (*Achillea ptarmica* 'The Pearl')
4. 'Blanc Double de Coubert' rugosa rose (*Rosa rugosa* 'Blanc Double de Coubert')
5. Dame's rocket or sweet rocket (*Hesperis matronalis*)
6. Formosa lily (*Lilium formosanum*)
7. Scabious (*Scabiosa* × 'Butterfly Blue')
8. White scabious (*Scabiosa caucasica* 'Alba')
9. White martagon lilies (*Lilium martagon* 'Album')
10. Regal trumpet lily (*Lilium regale*)
11. Flowering tobacco (*Nicotiana sylvestris*)
12. White alpine pinks (*Dianthus alpinus* var. *albus*)
13. Night-flowering stock (*Mathiola bicornis*)
14. 'Casa Blanca' hybrid oriental lily (*Lilium* × 'Casa Blanca')

Hot Color Garden

The intensity of hot colors—saturated reds, vivid oranges, and bright yellows—demands attention. In the garden, where cooler, paler colors often reign, the vision of masses of hot colors immediately captures both the eye and the imagination of the visitor.

This hot color garden, a long oval bed, has been designed to stand alone as a fiery island of hot color surrounded by a cool green lawn. A tall, pyramidal, or conical evergreen is positioned off center to serve as a visual anchor to the bed, which might appear to float in the landscape without this sturdy green weight.

Though the plant list includes only eleven different species, the choice of two reblooming cultivars of daylilies and three yarrow cultivars creates a bloom period that lasts from May through October.

Adding late-winter- and spring-blooming bulbs such as winter aconite will bring color to the bed as early as February. Planting various types of daffodils in shades of yellow and orange, along with orange, red, and yellow tulips will build the "heat" in March, April, and early May.

In order to fill in spaces of developing shrubs and perennials and to ensure a lush, full bed, you may choose to add hot-colored annuals to your garden. Among the choices appropriate in this garden are California and Iceland poppies, portulaca, cosmos, and snapdragons.

To provide contrast to the hot colors, this design makes extensive use of white flowers, including 'White Swan' coneflowers and a white valerian cultivar called 'Snowcloud'. You might also wish to add or substitute a white butterfly weed, *Asclepias incarnata* 'Ice Ballet', which, like its orange and red cousin, blooms through June and July. In addition to pleasing contrasts, the white flowers offer a visual "rest" and a good transition between patches of bright color

It is important to remember that varying shades of green are also useful to prevent the bold colors in a hot color garden from becoming overbearing. In this design, large clumps of yellow flag iris (*Iris pseudacorus*) are placed throughout the bed. Though their bloom period is relatively short, the swordlike blue-green foliage makes a particularly attractive foil for the hot colors of later-blooming plants. Daylily foliage and the silvery green feathers of yarrow leaves also provide a little visual calm in this intense planting scheme.

The mix of reds, oranges and yellows with soothing greens and white gives this bed great impact for its small size. Best of all, once established these perennials need little attention.

'Goblin' blanket flower

A Border for an Island Bed

An island bed placed within a verdant lawn is a visual treat in any landscape. To keep the bed looking its best, it is important that the surrounding lawn be mowed regularly. But mowing can pose problems for plants placed along the edges of the bed. Part of the charm of the plants chosen for this design is their wonderfully diverse forms, which include sprawling and spreading inclinations. In order to protect foliage and bloom from potential damage by mower blades, this garden bed would be well served by a stone, cement paver, or brick edging path.

Any one of several path materials would be appropriate for this situation. The simplest path involves encircling the bed with a span of pea gravel, though this necessitates a retaining edge on either side to keep the gravel from spreading out into the lawn and the bed.

Two courses of bricks laid end to end from the edge of the bed make an especially attractive protective ring. Square flagstones, a crazy paving of broken stones, precast concrete blocks, or interlocking blocks would all work equally well.

If none of these options fits within your budget, a deep edging of at least two inches' width made with an edging tool or a sharp spade will provide the plantings with some protection from the mower.

Hot Color Garden Plant List

1. Yellow flag iris (*Iris pseudacorus*)
2. 'Moerheim Beauty' sneezeweed (*Helenium* 'Moerheim Beauty')
3. 'Snowcloud' valerian (*Centranthus ruber* 'Snowcloud')
4. 'Happy Returns' daylily (*Hemerocallis* 'Happy Returns')
5. 'Fire Flames' cinquefoil (*Potentilla atrosanguinea* 'Fire Flames')
6. 'Moonbeam' tickseed (*Coreopsis verticillata* 'Moonbeam')
7. 'Fireland' yarrow (*Achillea millefolium* 'Fireland')
8. 'Crimson Beauty' yarrow (*Achillea millefolium* 'Crimson Beauty')
9. 'White Swan' coneflower (*Echinacea purpurea* 'White Swan')
10. 'Red Chief' red hot poker (*Kniphofia uvaria* 'Red Chief')
11. 'Red Reward' daylily (*Hemerocallis* 'Red Reward')
12. 'Goblin' blanket flower (*Gaillardia* 'Goblin')
13. 'Gay Butterflies' butterfly weed (*Asclepias tuberosa* 'Gay Butterflies')
14. 'Coronation Gold' yarrow (*Achillea millefolium* 'Coronation Gold')
15. Leyland cypress (*Cupressocyparis lelandii*)

Hummingbird Garden

There are few creatures more fascinating to observe than hummingbirds. Their irrepressible natures, the curious humming sound made by their rapidly beating wings, and the brilliant coloring of the males—along with their unique ability to hover and fly backwards, sideways, and straight up or down—combine to make a wondrous show. The more you learn about hummingbirds, moreover, the more extraordinary they seem. The only hummingbird that nests east of the Mississippi, for example, is the ruby-throated hummingbird (*Archiloctius colubris*). This species winters anywhere from northern Mexico and southern Texas south to Costa Rica, yet this diminutive creature (it is only three to four inches [7 to 10cm] in length) nevertheless manages to fly up to six hundred miles, across the Gulf of Mexico, as it migrates east in the spring and summer.

While a few of the 341 known species of hummingbird subsist on a diet of insects exclusively, most species rely heavily on flower nectar as well as insects and spiders. In this hummingbird garden design, many of those nectar sources are combined in such a way as to be not only appealing to hummingbirds but aesthetically satisfying as well. Also included are cinnamon ferns, a source of nesting material, and a large rock in the shade, which will encourage lichens (also used in hummingbird nests).

Wild columbine

The best way to attract hummingbirds to your garden is to use a diversity of nectar-rich plants that bloom at different times. The birds need a great deal of food in the spring to enable them to complete in good health their arduous journey from their winter homes. Spring-flowering nectar sources are thus critical, and this plan includes azaleas, Carolina rhododendron, blueberry, lilac, a May-blooming perennial sage, honeysuckle, Japanese iris, red buckeye, and a great mass of wild columbine, which is particularly beloved by hummingbirds. These little birds continue to feed heavily through the late spring and summer, and can feast in this garden on the trumpet vine that will quickly cover the pergola, as well as on daylilies, beard tongue, larkspur, Turk's cap lily, agastache, summer phlox, bee balm, sweet azalea, dwarf glossy abelia, catmint, fuchsia, sage, and long-flowered gilly. Two hummingbird feeders are also included because they are, if well cared for, a great source of quick energy for these active birds (see Caring for a Hummingbird Feeder on page 44).

In autumn, before the weather turns cold, most hummingbirds will once again set out on the long voyage back to their winter nests. This is when it is especially important to provide nectar sources and to keep your feeders full. The late-flowering sages are perfect because they are a rich source of food

as well as a glorious finale for the garden, blooming in brilliant shades of red, blue, and purple. Also in bloom in autumn in this garden is crepe myrtle, cardinal flower, and the agastache, catmint, and fuchsia, which have already been flowering for many months. The cardinal flowers, as well as the cinnamon ferns and Japanese irises, are not drought-tolerant and should only be planted where they will stay reliably moist through the heat of summer.

There are not a great many bulbs that provide nectar for hummingbirds—Turk's cap lilies, tiger lilies, gladioli, daylilies, and irises essentially complete the list. Additional bulbs are recommended in this design not as a potential food source but strictly for their ornamental value in early spring.

Hummingbirds have a special fondness for red and have been known to probe with terrific curiosity, and probably considerable disappointment, red neckties, scarves, hats, and even red buttons on cameras. More appealing would surely be the red-flowering plants included here, notably red buckeye, wild columbine, red trumpet vine (which has the tubular-shaped flowers so ideally suited to the hummingbirds' anatomy), red daylily cutivars, a red form of honeysuckle and of summer phlox, cardinal flowers, a red- and purple-flowered fuchsia, and a scarlet-colored cultivar of long-flowered gilly.

A garden designed for hummingbirds should have a wealth not only of nectar sources, but also of places to roost and shelter. As tough and feisty as these creatures are known to be, they do need somewhere to go in the event of a driving rainstorm or fierce winds. The woody plants used here—red buckeye, lilac, sweet azalea, Carolina rhododendron, the azalea cultivar known as 'Koromo Shikibu', and crepe myrtle—serve both as an important food source when they are in bloom and as safe perches in inclement weather.

Caring for a Hummingbird Feeder

Your feeder will be most effective in attracting hummingbirds if you are careful about what you put in your feeder, and if you keep it well filled and make sure it is clean. Here are a few guidelines that will help keep the hummingbirds you attract healthy and happy:

1. Clean your feeder often, along with any bottles or other containers in which you store hummingbird food.

2. Nectar solutions more than a few days old should be discarded. While most hummingbirds have the sense to avoid aged solutions, some do not. If a hummer drinks from a sugar-water solution that has already gone bad, it can become temporarily disoriented and thus an easy prey for predators. A fermented honey-water solution can even cause a fatal fungal disease. It is best not to ever use honey in hummingbird feeders.

3. The sugar-water solution you use should be no stronger than one part sugar to four parts water, since too much sugar can potentially cause liver damage. Boil the water you use in the solution for two or three minutes to kill all bacteria. The water should also be as free of chemicals as possible.

4. Use a bright red feeder to attract the birds rather than adding food dye to your nectar solution; the dye can be harmful to the birds.

5. Placing the feeder in shade, or at least in partial shade, will keep the solution from going bad too quickly. Always clean the feeder thoroughly before refilling it.

6. Try not to let the feeder sit empty for more than a day or two or the hummingbirds you have managed to attract may become discouraged and go elsewhere.

7. Set your feeder out in spring when the hummingbirds first start to appear in your area; the timing will vary by region. Watch the early-blooming perennials and shrubs—especially azaleas, flowering quince, columbine, and woodland phlox—to determine when the hummingbirds will arrive. Take your feeder in when the birds in your area have historically tended to leave; a hummingbird that stays behind when it should logically migrate may well perish in the cold.

The maintenance requirements of this garden are by no means burdensome. The trumpet vine should have more than enough room to grow contentedly over the pergola without pruning, though the honeysuckle growing up the post in the garden is best cut back hard in early spring. An effective way to train this honeysuckle is to wrap the post, before planting, with black deer fencing. If the post is painted black, the fencing will be visible only at close range, and will virtually disappear once the vine starts its vigorous growth.

Only the Turk's cap lily and the larkspur are likely to require staking; this should be done in the spring or very early summer, before the task becomes too formidable. Perennials likely to flower again later in the summer, for instance the catmint and 'May Night' sage, should be seriously sheared back after the first strong flush of bloom. Keep an eye on the bee balm, too, because it does have a tendency to run quite aggressively through the garden. This propensity to romp, not to mention the powdery mildew that inevitably covers even those bee balm cultivars sworn to be mildew-resistant, may cause you to think twice about including this plant in your garden. But once you've seen how hummingbirds flock to it—at times swarming over the bee balm so thickly that the whole garden seems extraordinarily vibrant and alive—well, at that point all common sense is abandoned.

With a little planning and maintenance, you can transform your backyard into a haven for these charming little birds. In addition, you'll be creating a garden that you and your family will enjoy almost as much as your winged guests.

ADDITIONAL NECTAR PLANTS

This hummingbird garden design is not meant to be all-encompassing, and you may wish to substitute some other hummingbird-attracting plants for those included here. If you live in a warm region there is a vast array of tropical plants that could be included—pentas, lantana, agapanthus, scarlet bush, orange tree, and tree tobacco, for example. In a more temperate region you can still grow these plants, but they may best be considered annuals. In a temperate climate you can, however, reliably plant a great many perennials and woody plants beyond what is included here, notably butterfly bush, beauty bush, rose of Sharon, weigela, winter currant, winter jasmine, hollyhock, red-hot poker, and Virginia bluebell, to name just a few.

Red-hot poker

NECTAR SOURCES: STRAIGHT SPECIES VERSUS CULTIVARS

So many new cultivars of woody and herbaceous plants are introduced to the public each year that not even the most obsessive plant collector could hope to keep up. There are, for example, hundreds of daylily cultivars now being sold and scores more sure to be available with each passing year. But plant breeders may not necessarily be working in a direction that is most beneficial to wildlife. They may be breeding for different flower color or size or some other aesthetic attribute, or for better disease-resistance, or for a myriad of other qualities. Whether or not the new cultivated form is rich in nectar is not generally a consideration. This is not to say that all cultivars are nectar-deprived but rather that you should not assume that all cultivars have the same quality and/or quantity of nectar as is likely to be found in the straight species of the same plant. Some cultivars of hummingbird plants will prove to be just as popular with the birds as the straight species, while others will turn out to be so lacking in nectar as to be useless in a garden specifically designed to attract hummingbirds. What this means is that the intrepid gardener will have to do some experimenting to determine which cultivars of which plants are good nectar sources. Or you could, when in doubt, accept some potential ornamental shortcomings and stick to the straight species.

Cardinal flower

Hummingbird Garden Plant List

1. 'Koromo Shikibu' evergreen azalea (*Rhododendron* 'Koromo Shikibu')
2. Blunt-lobed woodsia (*Woodsia obtusa*)
3. Wild columbine (*Aquilegia canadensis*)
4. Blue columbine (*Aquilegia alpina*)
5. 'Royal Robe' cardinal flower (*Lobelia cardinalis* 'Royal Robe')
6. 'Crimson Trumpet' trumpet vine (*Campsis radicans* 'Crimson Trumpet')
7. Cinnamon fern (*Osmunda cinnamomea*)
8. Terra-cotta pot with fuchsias (*Fuchsia* 'Little Beauty' and *Fuchsia* 'Gartenmeister') and lobelia (*Lobelia erinus* 'Flore plena')
9. Red buckeye (*Aesculus pavia*)
10. 'Top Hat' dwarf blueberry (*Vaccineum* 'Top Hat')
11. 'Walker's Low' catmint (*Nepeta faassenii* 'Walker's Low')
12. 'Hummingbird Mix' long-flowered gilly (*Ipomopsis longiflora* 'Hummingbird Mix')
13. 'Prairie Night' bee balm (*Monarda didyma* 'Prairie Night')
14. Sweet azalea (*Rhododendron arborescens*)
15. Carolina rhododendron (*Rhododendron carolinianum*)
16. 'Miss Kim' lilac (*Syringa patula* 'Miss Kim')
17. 'Pardon Me' daylily (*Hemerocallis* 'Pardon Me')
18. 'Prostrata' dwarf glossy abelia (*Abelia × grandiflora* 'Prostrata')
19. 'May Night' sage (*Salvia × sylvestris* 'May Night')
20. 'Sandra' summer phlox (*Phlox paniculata* 'Sandra')
21. 'Husker Red' beard tongue (*Penstemon digitalis* 'Husker Red')
22. 'Blue Dawn' larkspur (*Delphinium* 'Blue Dawn')
23. Turk's cap lily (*Lilium superbum*)
24. 'Argentine Skies' sage (*Salvia guarnitica* 'Argentine Skies')
25. 'Firebird' agastache (*Agastache coccinea × rupestris* 'Firebird')
26. 'Shei Shonogan' Japanese iris (*Iris ensata* 'Shei Shonogan')
27. 'Cedar Lane' trumpet honeysuckle (*Lonicera sempervirens* 'Cedar Lane')
28. 'Red Reward' daylily (*Hemerocallis* 'Red Reward')
29. 'Yuma' crepe myrtle (*Lagerstroemia* 'Yuma')

You may also wish to include some spring-flowering bulbs to extend the bloom season

Winter aconite (*Eranthis cilicica*)
'Red Shine' tulip (*Tulipa* 'Red Shine')
'Trevithian' daffodil (*Narcissus* 'Trevithian')
'Sky Beauty' Dutch iris (*Iris xiphion* 'Sky Beauty')
'Tahiti' daffodil (*Narcissus* 'Tahiti')
'Danube' Spanish bluebell (*Hyacinthoides hispanica* 'Danube')
Like a lark (*Corydalis solida*)
True scilla (*Scilla bifolia*)
'Viridi-apice' snowdrop (*Galanthus nivalis* 'Viridi-apice')

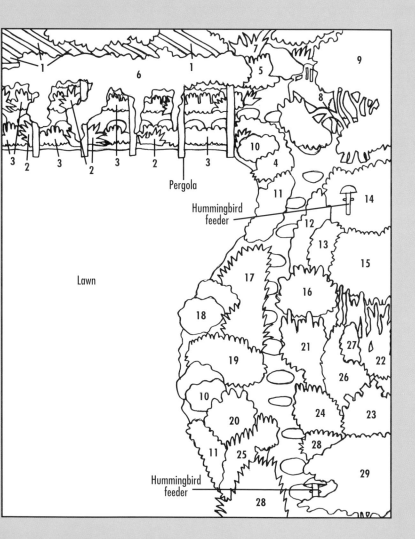

Backyard Meadow Garden

There is a certain romance to a meadow that is hard to define—when we think of "the country" we imagine fields of grasses dotted with brightly colored wildflowers. As more and more of the rural landscape disappears, there is growing interest in recapturing the wild feel of a sunny meadow in our urban and suburban backyards. This no doubt explains the terrific popularity of the so-called "meadow in a can." But while the exuberance of a meadow is aesthetically appealing, it is not always easy to re-create on a small scale. Many typical meadow plants are, in fact, quite large and/or thug-like, and not particularly well suited to a garden setting. Many of these seem, when viewed at close range, remarkably coarse. How, then, can we achieve the sensibility of a meadow without begetting what looks like a garden of weeds?

The artistry comes in choosing the right kinds of plants for your meadow garden and placing them with great care. In this design the emphasis is on plants that *evoke* a meadow rather than a strict adherence to plants native to such an environment. In many cases a cultivar is used instead of the straight species because the cultivar is more refined or restrained or aesthetically superior. Joe-Pye weed, for example, is commonplace in eastern meadows and is not especially remarkable. The cultivar known as 'Gateway', on the other hand, was chosen for its

Pale purple coneflower

bright red stems and dusky rose flowerheads and is quite spectacular. Our native switch grass is an interesting though not beautiful plant, but the cultivar of switch grass called 'Heavy Metal' has powder blue leaves and an upright habit, and is invaluable in the garden.

Several different kinds of grasses are woven throughout this garden design. The grasses, more than any other kind of plant, suggest by their form, texture, color, and movement the sense of a meadow. They are stunning when backlit by the sun and give an appearance of warmth and structure to the garden in winter.

The image of a meadow invariably conjures up pictures of birds and butterflies flitting across open, sunny spaces, taking advantage of the flower nectar and fruits to be found there. Indeed, one of the most magical elements of a meadow is that it seems so absolutely full of life. Many of the plants in this design were selected specifically because of their appeal to beneficial wildlife, including blue salvia, New England aster, Brazilian verbena, butterfly weed, butterfly bush, Joe-Pye weed, black-eyed Susan, coneflower, beard tongue, sneezeweed, yarrow, and goldenrod. Bird feeders on tall posts are included in two of the corners of the garden to provide a safe and reliable food source for birds, whatever the season.

Perhaps it is a function of the light or bright colors of late-season plants like asters, but meadows tend to be most glorious in summer and autumn. This backyard meadow design is definitely at its peak from late June through November. But this is not to say that the garden is unattractive or uninteresting at other times of the year. If the grasses are not cut back after frost, for instance, their straw color and the haunting sound as they sway in the wind are captivating in the gray months of winter. In spring the garden comes alive again with great masses of daffodils, the bright blue flowers of camassia, and the brilliant red flowers of poppies that have been seeded in late in the winter.

This backyard meadow is laid out in such a way as to give a sense of the plants growing naturally. The design calls for the meadow garden to be surrounded by a mowed lawn, and the path through the center of the garden is meant to be mowed as well—this border of cut lawn prevents the meadow garden from appearing unkempt. The path is narrow and discreet and at certain times of the year, when the plants have reached their mature size, it may well be totally invisible from certain angles. Many of the plants used along the path are large and lush to give one the feeling, when walking through the garden, of being enveloped by the meadow's sights, sounds, and scents.

A meadow garden may look care-free but it does require some attention to look its best. Weeds need to be kept under control or they can overwhelm such a garden. When weeding is done frequently it can be done by hand.

Several of the late-blooming plants will look most attractive if they are pinched back to half their size one or two times in late spring. This is the case with Joe-Pye weed, New England aster, sneezeweed, and sedum. The salvia will bloom from May until frost if sheared back after the first great flush of bloom and

periodically deadheaded thereafter. The black-eyed Susans, coneflowers, and beard tongue need not be deadheaded because their seedheads are both attractive and appealing to birds.

If the grasses are left up through the winter they must be cut back as far as possible in early spring, certainly before the new growth begins. The butterfly bush should also be cut back at this point to about six inches (15cm). If you leave the grasses and other perennials standing through the winter, when they can indeed look beautiful, make sure that you clear a few paths for predatory birds and animals, which will keep any rodent population in check.

DIVIDING ORNAMENTAL GRASSES

Like most herbaceous perennials, ornamental grasses will benefit greatly from being dug up and divided every few years. How often a grass needs to be divided depends upon the species. Fescues, for example, should be divided every three or four years. Most *Miscanthus* species need to be divided only after five to seven years. You can see clearly that your plant needs to be divided when it starts to open up in the center. Dig the grass up after it has started to grow again in the spring (dividing it while still dormant may kill it), discard the woody center, and create new divisions from the outside. Be sure that each new plant has at least five stems (known as "culms" in grasses). Replant the divisions right away and make sure they are well watered.

Seeding in Annuals

Starting annual and vegetable seeds indoors in winter is a great way to prepare for the coming spring and to ease winter's gloom. Some annuals, however, will do as well or better if their seeds are sown directly in the garden. Most seed packages will tell you whether the seeds should be sown directly outdoors or started inside. Poppies, cosmos, larkspur, and cleome, for example, all tend to become quite spindly when grown indoors under artificial light. Even if you are diligent about pinching them back, they do not always respond well to being transplanted come spring. If you sow their seeds directly in the garden, on the other hand, they seem to get off to a better start.

Once you have established that your seeds should be sown directly you need to make sure that the soil in your garden is neither compacted from the winter nor nutrient-deprived. If it needs to be tilled a bit to loosen it or if organic material needs to be added this should be done before you sow any seeds. Also be sure that you are sowing at the correct time for your specific seeds. Poppies, for instance, should be sown in late winter or early autumn. Other annuals are more cold-sensitive and should be sown closer to the last frost date in your region. Try to keep the area you have seeded free of weeds, otherwise it can be difficult to distinguish the annual seedlings from the weeds when they start to grow. Once they grow it is essential, though painful, to thin the seedlings. If the tiny plants are overly crowded they will grow only weakly. Thin the seedlings when they are still small so that the remaining plants have a chance to grow into bushy, healthy specimens.

Backyard Meadow Garden Plant List

1. 'Chameleon' purple spurge (*Euphorbia dulcis* 'Chameleon')
2. Brazilian verbena (*Verbena bonariensis*)
3. 'Purple Dome' New England aster (*Aster novae-angliae* 'Purple Dome')
4. 'Premium Yellow' butterfly weed (*Asclepias incarnata* 'Premium Yellow')
5. 'Gateway' Joe-Pye weed (*Eupatorium fistulosum* 'Gateway')
6. Arkansas amsonia (*Amsonia hubrechtii*)
7. 'Cassian' fountain grass (*Pennisetum alopecuroides* 'Cassian')
8. 'Karl Foerster' feather reed grass (*Calamagrostis* × *acutiflora* 'Karl Foerster')
9. 'Rachel's Eyes' black-eyed Susan (*Rudbeckia fulgida* var. *fulgida* 'Rachel's Eyes')
10. 'Bruno' sneezeweed (*Helenium autumnale* 'Bruno')
11. Pale purple coneflower (*Echinacea pallida*)
12. 'Fireland' yarrow (*Achillea filipendulina* 'Fireland')
13. 'Blue Fortune' anise hyssop (*Agastache foeniculum* 'Blue Fortune')
14. 'The Blues' little bluestem (*Schizochyrium scoparium* 'The Blues')
15. 'Prince' calico aster (*Aster lateriflorus* 'Prince')
16. 'Blue Hill' blue salvia (*Salvia superba* 'Blue Hill')
17. Butterfly weed (*Asclepias tuberosa*)
18. 'Black Knight' butterfly bush (*Buddleia davidii* 'Black Knight')
19. 'Heavy Metal' blue switch grass (*Panicum virgatum* 'Heavy Metal')
20. 'Fireworks' dwarf rough-leaved goldenrod (*Solidago rugosa* 'Fireworks')
21. 'Husker Red' burgundy-foliage beard tongue (*Penstemon digitalis* 'Husker Red')
22. 'Mohrchen' burgundy-leaved stonecrop (*Sedum* 'Mohrchen')
23. Scottish tufted hair grass (*Deschampsia caespitosa* 'Schottland')

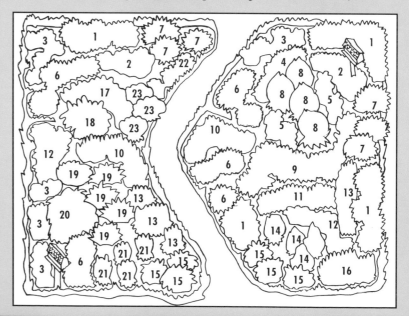

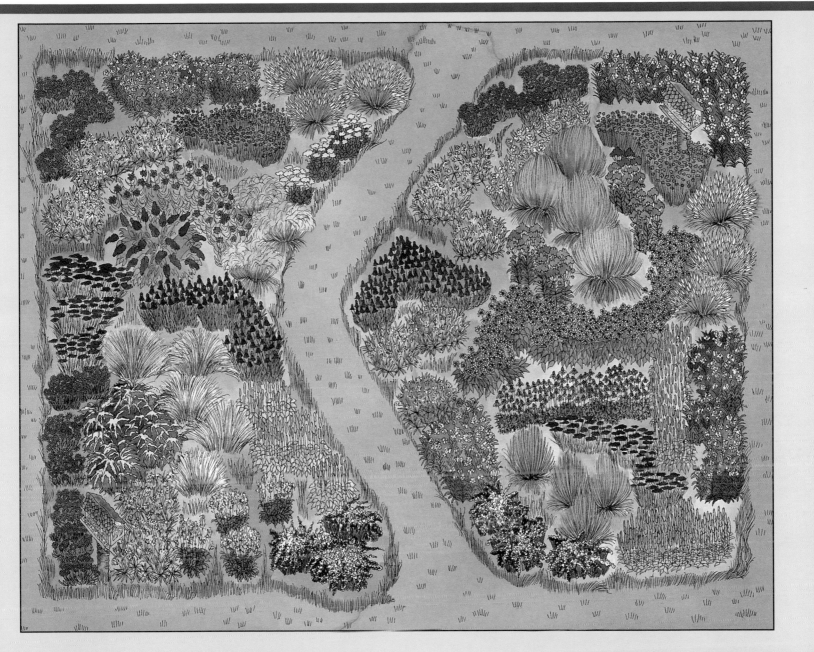

NOTES

Plant globe thistle (*Echinops ritro* 'Veitch's Blue') here and there through the center of the garden.

Poppies (*Papaver somniferum*) should be seeded in throughout.

INCLUDE THE FOLLOWING BULBS, SCATTERED THROUGHOUT THE MEADOW IN DRIFTS

'Carlton' daffodil (*Narcissus* 'Carlton')

'Mint Julep' daffodil (*Narcissus* 'Mint Julep')

Giant allium (*Allium giganteum*) (Plant among the larger grasses to hide the dying foliage.)

'Blue Danube' camassia (*Camassia leichtlinii* 'Blue Danube')

Backyard Wetland

Not everyone is lucky enough to have a pond, stream, or water garden in their backyard. Garden centers and catalogs are quickly catching on to this craze, though, and soon it will be as easy to install a water garden on your deck or in your yard as it is to plant a container of flowers. If you already have a water feature in your landscape, this "wetland" garden will work nicely alongside it. For those whose water gardens are still distant dreams, odds are there is a spot in your yard where water accumulates in the soil, creating a miniature bog or wetland. Instead of letting these boglike spots become mosquito resorts, make the most of a bad situation by planting a garden of water-loving trees, shrubs, and perennials.

Water is necessary to all plants, but three types are especially adaptable to wet conditions: plants that will thrive in wet, boggy areas with standing water; plants that require soil that is evenly moist but well drained and without standing water; and plants that will grow in ponds and water gardens. Plants that thrive in wetlands are rapidly losing their natural habitat as wetlands are reclaimed for agricultural or industrial use, or are built up for housing developments.

In a residential lot, a "wetland" is a depressed area where water collects or any area that floods regularly and doesn't drain quickly. Amend the soil with peat, shredded leaves, compost, or sand but keep additional topsoil to a minimum so that you don't raise the grade and change drainage patterns. To increase the water level in your wetland, install underground piping that will aim the water from gutters and sump pumps toward the wetland. Areas that flood severely may be helped by the installation of underground drain tiles or a sloping grade that will divert the flow of rainwater.

Queen-of-the-prairie

If your "wetland" or water garden includes sufficient water to accommodate fish, do a little research before purchasing any watery friends. Many varieties of fish will demolish plants in the water or along the water's edge. Make sure that any fish you introduce to the wetland will live in harmony with the plants that share their space.

If you choose not to add fish to your watery ecosystem, it does not mean the plants will have the wetland to themselves. Depending on the region where you live, you may find butterflies, frogs, toads, and assorted amphibians, plus a wide variety of birds, setting up home in your backyard. Any mosquito-eating visitors are welcome additions to a wetland garden, and should be encouraged with plants that they enjoy.

With just a bit of planning you can transform your boggy backyard into a wetland garden for all to enjoy.

TREES FOR WETLANDS

Most wetland areas are in at least partial shade, since direct sunlight would eventually dry them out. If you are creating a wetland or taking a slightly boggy area and expanding it, be sure to include a few trees or large shrubs that will provide filtered shade. Trees that like wet areas include dawn redwood (*Metasequoia glyptostroboides;* needs moist but well-drained soil); sweet bay (*Magnolia virginiana*); red maple (*Acer rubrum*); sweet gum (*Liquidambar styraciflua*); river birch (*Betula nigra;* can survive standing water); balsam fir (*Abies balsamea*); striped maple (*Acer pensylvanicum*); mountain maple (*Acer spicatum*); Ohio buckeye (*Aesculus glabra*); northern catalpa (*Catalpa speciosa*); redbud (*Cercis candensis*); green ash (*Fraxinus pennsylvanica*); thornless honey locust (*Gleditsia triacanthos* var. *inermis;* also water locust, *Gleditsia aquatica*); Ozark witch hazel (*Hamamelis vernalis*); tulip tree (*Liriodendron tulipifera*); swamp tupelo and water tupelo (*Nyssa biflora* and *N. aquatica;* both suitable for southern climates); Pinckneya (*Pinckneya bracteata;* zone 7); willow (*Salix* spp.; be careful with this genus—willows grow very quickly and spread rapidly); and swamp cyrilla (*Cyrilla racemiflora*).

Moisture-loving shrubs include buttonbush (*Cephalanthus occidentalis*); snowberry (*Symphoricarpos* spp.); Allegheny serviceberry (*Amelanchier laevis*); winterberry (*Ilex verticillata;* a male pollinator is necessary to produce fruit); summersweet (*Clethra alnifolia;* also known as sweet pepperbush); sweetspire (*Itea virginica*); pussy willow (*Salix caprea*); swamp azalea (*Rhododendron viscosum*); variegated red twig dogwood (*Cornus alba* 'Elegantissima'); mountain laurel (*Kalmia latifolia*); spicebush (*Lindera benzoin*); rose bay (*Rhododendron maximum;* grows into a large shrub or small tree); guelder rose (*Viburnum opulus*); and highbush blueberry (*Vaccinium corymbosum*).

'Heritage' river birch bark

53

Perennials That Love Water

A surprising number of perennials thrive in moist, or even wet, soils, although relatively few of these can survive a winter of "wet feet"—with their roots in standing water. The plants listed below perform well in evenly moist, well-drained soil; the exceptions that will thrive in standing water are noted.

Arrowhead (*Sagittaria latifolia;* another form of arrowhead, *Sagittaria sagittifolia,* will thrive in standing water up to about 6 inches [15cm] deep)

Bottle gentian (*Gentiana andrewsii*)

Cardinal flower (*Lobelia cardinalis*)

Cinnamon fern (*Osmunda cinnamomea*)

False indigo (*Baptisia australis;* there is a totally different plant, good for wetland areas, also called false indigo but its botanical name is *Amorpha fruticosa*)

False spirea (*Astilbe* spp.)

Featherleaf rodgersia (*Rodgersia pinnata* 'Superba')

Globeflower (*Trollius* spp.)

Goat's beard (*Aruncus dioicus*)

Great lobelia (*Lobelia siphilitica*)

Hardy water canna (*Thalia dealbata*)

Jack-in-the-pulpit (*Arisaema triphyllum*)

Joe-Pye weed (*Eupatorium maculatum*)

Marsh marigold (*Caltha palustris*)

Moneywort (*Lysimachia nummularia*)

Ostrich fern (*Matteuccia struthiopteris*)

Primrose (*Primula* × *polyantha*)

Queen-of-the-prairie (*Filipendula rubra* 'Venusta')

Red milkweed (*Asclepias incarnata*)

Sedge (*Carex stricta*)

Snakeroot (*Cimicifuga racemosa*)

Snakeweed (*Polygonum bistorta* 'Superbum')

Swamp rose mallow (*Hibiscus moscheutos*)

Sweet flag (*Acoris calamus* 'Variegatus')

Turtlehead (*Chelone glabra, C. lyonii,* and *C. obliqua*)

Variegated ribbon grass (*Phalaris arundinacea* 'Picta')

Wild iris (*Iris versicolor*)

Yellow waxbells (*Kirengeshoma palmata*)

Marsh marigold

Backyard Wetland Plant List

1. 'Heritage' river birch (*Betula nigra* 'Heritage')
2. Westonbirt dogwood (*Cornus alba* 'Sibirica')
3. Dwarf European cranberrybush viburnum (*Viburnum opulus* 'Compactum')
4. Goat's beard (*Aruncus dioicus*)
5. False spirea (*Astilbe × arendsii* 'Peach Blossom')
6. Joe-Pye weed (*Eupatorium fistulosum*)
7. Queen-of-the-prairie (*Filipendula rubra* 'Venusta')
8. Cinnamon fern (*Osmunda cinnamomea*)
9. Ostrich fern (*Matteuccia struthiopteris*)
10. Pink summersweet (*Clethra alnifolia* 'Pink Spire')
11. Rose turtlehead (*Chelone lyonii*)
12. Dwarf astilbe (*Astilbe simplicifolia* 'Sprite')
13. Golden sedge (*Carex stricta* 'Bowles Golden')

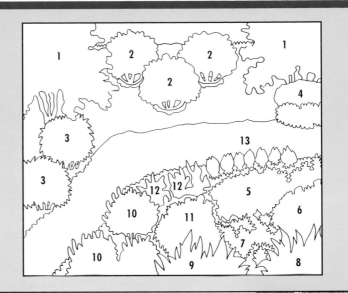

Streamside Garden

Few gardens are as romantic as those situated along the banks of a stream. Nature often provides her own beautiful landscape design by furnishing water-loving plants that thrive unbidden but welcomed. Sometimes an old willow will lose its tenuous grip on earth and fall across the stream, making a natural bridge, while ferns and mosses find a home in the rich organic matter of its decomposing root system.

But even nature's beauty can be improved upon. In this streamside garden, a tapestry of plants that enjoy the water's edge and some that prefer to have their feet totally submerged are layered along the length of the stream, unified by a thick carpet of moss covering both banks.

These plants have been selected first for their willingness to grow in moist or wet conditions. The second concern is to include a visually pleasing and stimulating variety of shapes, colors, and textures that will supply an ever-changing display over many months. Finally, this design uses hardy plant varieties that require minimal maintenance.

The yellow flag iris and its relative the pure blue water iris share the same straplike leaf shape in a beautiful shade of blue-green. These leaves play a leading role in this garden as they become a foil for other blooming plants once their own stunning flower performance is through. Contrasting foliage forms

Variegated blue water iris

come from the pickerelweed's arrow-shaped glossy leaves, feathery Japanese and royal ferns, and the small hearts of marsh marigold leaves.

Colors in this streamside retreat range from the vivid reds of cardinal flowers, which bloom for most of the summer, to the pink-white clouds of water plantain blossoms. The two ragwort cultivars add shades of yellow and orange to the palette, and 'Othello' boasts interesting bronze-red heart-shaped leaves as well. Rose pink flowering rush, pale pink European bistort, buttercup yellow marsh marigold flowers, and white plumes of goatsbeard add depth to the color scheme.

A bench occupies a coveted spot under the willow. Here, you can sit in the shade and watch the movement of the stream, lulled by the bubbling music. Two large stands of dwarf cattails are stationed on either side of the stream, bringing to the design a strong vertical form and providing late-season interest in the form of brown fuzzy cattails. This small species (growing only one to two feet [30.5 to 61cm]) is preferable to the larger species because it allows visitors seated on the bench to appreciate an unobstructed view from one side of the bank to the other. In addition, this diminutive species won't require the difficult maintenance task of yearly thinning.

Flat, smooth-edged stones create a walkway beneath the willow, leading to the bench and back to the house. Providing a path for foot traffic will protect the rather delicate moss from unnecessary trampling.

'The Rocket' ragwort

GROWING A MOSS LAWN

If your streamside garden does not have an existing moss lawn, it is possible to start one. Though it does take some effort and time, the reward of the rich, springy carpet of moss is worth the work it takes to create it. Here's how to do it:

1. Remove all vegetation from the area, including grass, roots, leaves, sticks, and twigs so you are left with bare soil.

2. Add an acidifying agent such as sulfur dust, aluminum sulfate, or ammonium sulfate to bring the pH of the soil to 5.5. Use a soil testing kit to ensure the proper pH.

3. Rake the soil so the top layer is crumbly but smooth.

4. Plant commercially grown moss (which is sold in flats) by laying it on top of the acidified soil and gently pressing it into the soil.

5. Water well. An alternative to planting commercially grown moss is to make a "moss soup."

MOSS SOUP

1. Prepare the soil as in Steps 1 through 3 above.

2. Find several clumps of moss on your property or that of a friend (never help yourself to moss from a park or from the side of the road. You should always have permission from the property owner first.)

3. Break up the moss and put it in your blender.

4. Add a cup of buttermilk or beer.

5. Blend.

6. Pour the mixture directly on the soil.

Keep the area moist with mist, not heavy watering, and wait for the moss to begin to grow. Eventually it will spread and colonize on its own. You can also pour the moss soup over large rocks or rotted tree stumps.

Yellow flag iris

ADDING STONES

Though many streamside gardens are naturally equipped with stones, you may need to import them in order to complete the design. Stones will also protect plantings and the stream's banks from heavy water flows produced by storms and winter thaws.

In this design, large rounded boulders have been placed at the curves along the stream bank. Rushing water is a powerful force and needs to be diverted. Here, the massive stones push the water away from the bank and direct its force toward the next boulder.

Always use local stone to "make it look like the rocks grew there," as one landscape designer suggests. The rocks should be heavily padded and carried in slings to protect them against damage when being transported from the quarry to their new home.

Incorporate smaller stones into the floor of the streambed, aligning them with the flow of the water. Place a few of the stones askew for a more natural look. If the stream dries up, as many do in the height of the summer, the stones along the dry bed provide a short-term visual substitute for the flowing water.

Streamside Garden Plant List

1. Marsh marigold (*Caltha palustris*)

2. Cardinal flower (*Lobelia cardinalis*)

3. Goatsbeard (*Aruncus doicus*)

4. Yellow flag iris (*Iris pseudacorus*)

5. 'Metallicum' Japanese painted fern (*Athyrium nipponicum* 'Metallicum')

6. Pickerelweed (*Pontederia cordata*)

7. Royal fern (*Osmunda regalis*)

8. European bistort (*Polygonum bistorta*)

9. Water plantain (*Alisma plantago* var. *aquatica*)

10. Blue water iris (*Iris laevigata*)

11. 'The Rocket' ragwort (*Ligularia stenocephala* 'The Rocket')

12. Dwarf cattail (*Typha minima*)

13. 'Othello' ragwort (*Ligularia dentata* 'Othello')

14. Weeping willow (*Salix babylonica*)

15. Daffodil (*Narcissus* spp.)

Seaside Garden

Set on a bluff above a small bay, this garden is designed to add color, texture, scent, and protection from wind to a seaside backyard during the summer months. Here, two free-form beds grace either side of a simple stone path that leads to the beach below the bluff.

Thick, hardy rugosa roses, with their distinctive, glossy, dark green leaves, are planted at the back of a berm set on the edge of the bluff. These wind-resistant, shrubby roses not only serve as a windbreak, but provide profuse, scented blooms in white and pink. The flowers are followed in autumn by vivid reddish hips. The hips, a rich source of vitamin C, can be used to make jelly and are also attractive to birds.

Blue tones are delivered by the low tufts of fescue, the silvery blue lavender leaves, and the intense blue spikes of 'Sunny Border Blue' speedwell, which blooms from midsummer through early autumn, especially if the spent flower spikes are removed.

'Hidcote' lavender strikes a deep purple note and is planted lushly for its wonderful scent as well as its silver foliage and distinct flower color. Lavender performs best when it is provided with a sand mulch and a bit of lime scratched into the soil around the base of each plant.

'Frau Dagmar Hartopp' rose

Reinforcing the pale pink of the rugosa rose 'Frau Dagmar Hartopp' is the strong rose-red of 'Magnus' coneflower. An additional pink tone—this one with a tinge of lilac—comes from the 'Apple Blossom' yarrow, a reliable, scented plant with silvery fernlike foliage. 'Apple Blossom' blooms from midsummer through early autumn, and will sometimes rebloom late in the autumn, a surprising and treasured bonus.

Sunny lemon yellow 'Happy Returns' daylilies provide contrast with the blues and purples, and offer a delicious scent as well. This repeat bloomer will have flowers from June through October and was selected over the more well-known golden yellow 'Stella d'Oro' daylily because of its softer color. Removing spent blooms encourages reblooming.

White flowers unify this garden scheme and come in the form of a repeat-blooming iris cultivar called 'Immortality', long-blooming candytuft, summer-blooming 'White Swan' coneflowers, and the white rugosa rose 'Blanc Double de Coubert'.

These hardy and beautiful plants are sure to flourish in your seaside garden, tolerating both gentle wind and salt air. With just a little planning you can have a beautiful garden that offers great color and form with a minimum of care.

Daylilies are stunning and hardy additions to the seaside garden.

CREATING A WINDBREAK

While this garden is designed for a relatively protected bayside property, seaside gardens are often very windy places. Most plants find it difficult to survive under severely windy conditions, which rob them of vital moisture and punish their limbs and leaves. If your seaside garden is in a very windy spot, you may find it necessary to create a windbreak to cut or divert the wind and protect the plants.

Building a berm—a mound or bank of earth—at the windward edge of the property is one of the options for creating a windbreak. You can construct a berm by moving or bringing in soil with heavy equipment to create a broad mound. To further protect the property from the wind, plant the berm densely with wind-tolerant trees and shrubs. You might also create a windbreak with a tall hedge of such trees or shrubs.

The following plants are appropriate for coastal, exposed, or windy sites:

TREES

Birch	Red cedar
Crab apple	Russian olive
English holly	Shadbush
Honey locust	Whitebeam
Japanese black pine	White spruce
Leyland cypress	

SHRUBS

Bayberry	Privet
Beach plum	Pussy willow
Potentilla	Mugho pine
Contoneaster	Roses (Rugosa and Gallica varieties)
Pyracantha	Summersweet (*Clethra*)
Forsythia	Tamarisk
Japanese barberry	Yew
Juniper 'Skyrocket'	Yucca
Lavender	

PERENNIALS AND GRASSES

Yarrow	Ribbon grass
Alyssum	Baby's breath
Rock cress	Daylilies
Thrift	Lythrum
Artemisia	Evening primrose
Butterfly bush	Poppy
Dianthus varieties	Potentilla
Gaillardia	Sedum
Northern sea oats grass	Lamb's ears
Dwarf pampas grass	Thyme
Panicum grass (also known as switch grass)	Veronica varieties
	Globe thistle

Evening primrose

SEASIDE GARDEN PLANT LIST

1. 'Little Gem' candytuft (*Iberis sempervirens* 'Little Gem')

2. 'Elijah Blue' fescue (*Festuca* 'Elijah Blue')

3. 'Frau Dagmar Hartopp' rose (*Rosa* 'Frau Dagmar Hartopp')

4. 'Blanc Double de Coubert' rose (*Rosa* 'Blanc Double de Coubert')

5. 'Happy Returns' daylily (*Hemerocallis* 'Happy Returns')

6. 'Magnus' purple coneflower (*Echinacea purpurea* 'Magnus')

7. 'Sunny Border Blue' speedwell (*Veronica* 'Sunny Border Blue')

8. 'White Swan' coneflower (*Echinacea purpurea* 'White Swan')

9. 'Immortality' iris (*Iris* 'Immortality')

10. 'Apple Blossom' yarrow (*Achillea millefolium* 'Apple Blossom')

11. 'Hidcote' lavender (*Lavandula angustifolia* 'Hidcote')

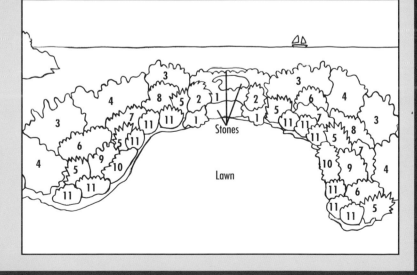

Water-Wise Garden

*I*n these days of restricted watering and frequent droughts (which often seem to follow weeks of rain and flooding) it makes sense to plant a garden that requires minimal supplemental watering. Bear in mind that the garden will need regular watering from the time it is planted until the plants become established (or until the plants have about tripled in size)—at least for several weeks, and even longer if the weather is particularly hot and dry. A periodic deep watering will help the roots develop. All transplants and seedlings need water, no matter how drought-tolerant they may become when they are older and established. Try not to install any new plantings in periods of restricted water use.

To get your water-wise garden off to a good start, install as many plants as possible in the autumn. This will give the plants a whole winter for the roots to develop and for the plants to become established in their new home. Water well as late as possible into the winter—and protect the plants with a loose straw mulch in the absence of snow cover. You'll also need to make sure the soil is well drained in order to avoid water collecting around the root zone.

Mulch is an essential part of a water-wise garden. It helps maintain an even soil temperature, helps retain existing moisture in the soil, discourages weeds, and protects plants from "heave and thaw" conditions throughout the winter. Finely shredded bark mulch applied to a depth of about three inches (7cm) will do the trick, but be careful not to mound the mulch up close to the trunks of trees or shrubs or around the base of perennials. Excessive mulch piled too closely can provide shelter for damaging rodents and can cause plants to rot. If plants have been mulched over for winter protection, be sure to rake the mulch back in early spring.

Consider creating a water-wise garden around a patio or deck. The patio or deck replaces lawn areas that require frequent watering, allowing for a low-water solution for the entire yard. When designing a large-scale water-wise garden, it is necessary to focus on plants that thrive in the area with little fuss. Native plants may fill this requirement if the conditions in your garden replicate the conditions of the plants' native habitat. A suburban lawn that was stripped of topsoil when the house was built and later spread with soil and grass seed or sod is unlikely to meet those conditions. Ornamental grasses, prairie grasses, and prairie flowers are often well-adapted to water-wise gardens, but remember that these plants are as widely variable in their growing needs as any other perennial. It is often beneficial to group the plants in small clumps based on their specific soil and watering needs.

'White Swan' white coneflower

Landscapes designed for wise use of water are sometimes referred to as "xeriscapes." The concept of a xeriscape garden goes much further than a garden of plants with minimal watering needs. In certain areas where drought is a constant, deadly reality, lawns may be entirely replaced with hardscapes, and gardens may feature only the least thirsty of plants. In other regions the drought-resistant garden is more of a desire than a necessity, and in some areas water-wise gardens are taken a step further to include plants that are fire-resistant. The extent or necessity of a water-wise garden may be determined by your region, your budget, your time, or your taste—feel free to adapt the plan for your needs. The extent to which you plant also depends on whether you need a small sampling of plants or a full-fledged landscape plan.

The featured plants in this water wise garden plan have performed well for me through several hot, dry summers in Chicago and Cincinnati, also surviving some serious extremes of winter weather. Across the Midwest and in most other regions, these plants should perform equally well. In the extreme heat and humidity of the deep South, I have heard that the compact daylily 'Black Eyed Stella' may perform better than 'Stella d'Oro'. Russian sage (*Perovskia atriplicifolia*) has earned kudos for its performance across several zones, including recognition as the Perennial Plant of the Year in 1995 by the Perennial Plant Association. This association is made up of growers and researchers across the United States and Canada, and Russian sage earned this honor with its performance across the North American continent.

IDENTIFYING WATER-WISE PLANTS

Call it "team colors"—many water-wise plants have identifying characteristics that even novice gardeners can spot easily. Fine hairs covering the surface of a leaf indicate a plant that is probably drought-tolerant. Foliage that is silver, gray, or white is another sign of a water-wise plant. A number of these plants originated on the dry, rocky soils of the Mediterranean, giving them an inherited tolerance of hot, arid conditions. Many aromatic herbs also fall into this category. A few plants with these telltale characteristics are listed below, along with the recognized country of origin, but don't forget—many other plants that don't fall into this category may still be extremely drought-tolerant.

Russian sage

Lamb's ear, woolly betony (*Stachys byzantina*), Caucasus to Iran

Lavender (*Lavandula angustifolia* and other species), Mediterranean

Mullein (*Verbascum bombyciferum*), Asia Minor

Rosemary (*Rosmarinus officinalis*), Mediterranean

Russian sage (*Perovskia atriplicifolia*), Afghanistan

Santolina, lavender cotton (*Santolina chamaecyparissus* and other species), western and central Mediterranean

Silver sage (*Salvia argentea* and other species), Mediterranean (southern Europe and North Africa)

Snow-in-summer (*Cerastium tomentosum*), mountains of Europe and western Asia

Thyme (*Thymus vulgaris* and other species), western Mediterranean

Wormwood (*Artemisia absinthium* and other species), Eurasia, North Africa

Yarrow (*Achillea tomentosa*), southwest Europe to central Italy

WATER-WISE GARDEN PLANT LIST

1. Russian sage (*Perovskia atriplicifolia*)
2. 'Morning Light' Japanese silver grass (*Miscanthus sinensis* 'Morning Light')
3. 'Stella d'Oro' compact daylily (*Hemerocallis* × 'Stella d'Oro')
4. 'White Spire' tall gayfeather (*Liatris scariosa* 'White Spire')
5. 'Blue Danube' Stokes' aster (*Stokesia laevis* 'Blue Danube')
6. 'White Swan' white coneflower (*Echinacea purpurea* 'White Swan')
7. 'Summer Sun' rough heliopsis (*Heliopsis scabra* 'Summer Sun')

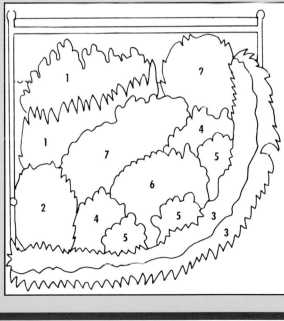

Sunny Garden

A sunny garden is one that will put a smile on your face—a daisy garden with lots of sunshiny yellow flowers—as well as a space featuring plants that thrive in full sun. This garden will be at its brightest and sunniest in late summer when the sneezeweed, false sunflowers, shasta daisies, daylilies, chrysanthemums, and ornamental grasses are all in flower at once. Earlier in the summer, the smaller 'Black Eyed Stella' daylilies and yarrow will hit their stride, with the dark purple foliage of 'Palace Purple' coral bells acting as a foil for the brighter colors in the garden.

A cheerful assortment of bulbs brightens the garden from early spring into the summer, and the emerging perennials will disguise the dying foliage of many of the bulbs. The brilliant stems of coral embers willows make the garden glow in winter, especially if the branches are cut down to about fifteen inches (38cm) every winter. The corneliancherry dogwood brings sunshine to the rainy days of spring, while the chokeberries attract birds into the garden with their red fruits and offer beautiful autumn color as well. Ornamental grasses add substance to the garden in winter, as will the distinct blue of the 'Fat Albert' spruce. Purple tones of the smokebush bring depth to the garden, and the smoky flowers enchant visitors when they open in late summer. The striking gold-tipped

'Alaska' shasta daisy

branches of the Oriental spruce provides a touch of sunshine to the garden in every season.

Extend the flowering season of the yarrow, sneezeweed, false sunflowers, shasta daisies, and chrysanthemums by removing flowers as soon as they are spent. Pinch back the chrysanthemums once or twice in early summer for a bushier bloom; for the best results in overwintering chrysanthemums, cut them back after frost and cover them with mulch, removing it in early spring. It is not necessary to deadhead the daylilies—the compact 'Black Eyed Stella' is a repeat bloomer that does not fade in the heat or sun, while the larger 'Ruby Throat' daylilies have a shorter period of bloom but with much more fanfare. Named after a type of hummingbird, this daylily should also attract its namesake. All the daisy-type flowers are ideal for cutting, and the yarrow also makes an excellent dried flower.

Once established, most of the plants in this garden require only moderate watering; the exception is the hedge of coral embers willow, which does best if the soil stays moist. In very dry areas, substitute a hedge of coral bark dogwoods—they also like moisture, but tend to hold up better than the willows in dry situations. A moderate fertilization of the perennial garden—two or three times in early summer—should be sufficient to keep the garden in its prime. Mulch all beds to retain moisture and keep out weeds—shredded leaves or shredded bark work nicely. Keep the mulch away from the base of the plants and don't install it deeper than three inches (7cm). Mow the lawn fairly high, to three to four inches (7 to 10cm), to keep it from drying out in midsummer—a lush, green lawn makes the yellow flowers look even sunnier.

When the garden is basking in the sun, park yourself on an Adirondack chair right in the middle of the lawn with a big straw hat, a tall cool glass of lemonade, and an Agatha Christie mystery. Close your eyes—just for a second—and feel the sun filtering through the brim of your hat. The garden chores will still be waiting later, but sunny summer afternoons are fleeting. The most important thing to remember about your sunny garden is to allow some time to enjoy it.

DROUGHT-TOLERANT PERENNIALS

Many sun-loving plants are also drought-tolerant, an important consideration when so many areas have watering restrictions in summer. Following are a few recommended plants for dry situations—you may wish to experiment with these if you live in an area with low rainfall.

- Evening primrose, sundrops (*Oenothera* spp.)
- Purple coneflower (*Echinacea purpurea*)
- Russian sage (*Perovskia atriplicifolia*)
- Wormwood (*Artemisia* spp.)
- Siberian forget-me-not (*Brunnera macrophylla*)
- Tickseed (*Coreopsis* spp.)
- Globe thistle (*Echinops ritro*)
- Indian blanketflower (*Gaillardia* × *grandiflora*)
- Lavender (*Lavandula angustifolia*)
- Gayfeather (*Liatris spicata*)
- Catmint (*Nepeta faassenii*)
- Beard tongue (*Penstemon* spp.)
- Pincushion flower (*Scabiosa caucasica*)
- Dusty miller (*Senecio cineraria*)
- Indian pink (*Silene laciniata*)
- Lamb's ears (*Stachys byzantina*)
- Vervain (*Verbena bonariensis*)
- Speedwell (*Veronica* spp.)
- Spanish bayonet (*Yucca filamentosa*)

Sunny Garden Plant List

1. 'Britzensis' coral embers willow (*Salix alba* 'Britzensis')
2. 'Fat Albert' Colorado blue spruce (*Picea pungens* 'Fat Albert')
3. 'Summer Sun' false sunflower (*Heliopsis helianthoides* 'Summer Sun')
4. 'Brilliant' sneezeweed (*Helenium autumnale* 'Brilliant')
5. 'Royal Purple' purple smoke bush (*Cotinus coggygria* 'Royal Purple', syn. 'Kromhout')
6. 'Happy Face' chrysanthemum (*Dendranthema × grandiflorum* 'Happy Face')
7. 'Alaska' shasta daisy (*Leucanthemum × superbum* 'Alaska')
8. 'Terra Cotta' yarrow (*Achillea millefolium* 'Terra Cotta')
9. 'Karl Foerster' feather reed grass (*Calamagrostis × acutiflora* 'Karl Foerster')
10. 'Palace Purple' purple-leaf coral bells (*Heuchera micrantha* 'Palace Purple')
11. 'Black Eyed Stella' compact daylily (*Hemerocallis × 'Black Eyed Stella')
12. 'Skylands' golden Oriental spruce (*Picea orientalis* 'Skylands')
13. 'Brilliantissima' red chokeberry (*Aronia arbutifolia* 'Brilliantissima')
14. 'Golden Glory' corneliancherry dogwood (*Cornus mas* 'Golden Glory')
15. 'Ruby Throat' daylily (*Hemerocallis × 'Ruby Throat')
16. Blue oat grass (*Helictotrichon sempervirens*)
17. 'Illusion' chrysanthemum (*Dendranthema × grandiflorum* 'Illusion')

Extend your bloom season by underplanting with bulbs

'Ming Yellow' hybrid oriental lily (*Lilium × 'Ming Yellow')—planted under sneezeweed

Winter aconites (*Eranthis cilicia*)—planted under smokebush and red chokeberries

'Blue Spike' grape hyacinths (*Muscari armeniacum* 'Blue Spike')—planted in tree circle under corneliancherry dogwood

'Manley' double-flowered daffodils (*Narcissus × 'Manley')—planted under 'Ruby Throat' daylilies and shasta daisies

'Minnow' miniature daffodils (*Narcissus × 'Minnow') planted under 'Black Eyed Stella' daylilies

'Mount Hood' trumpet daffodils (*Narcissus × 'Mount Hood') planted under chrysanthemums

'Angélique', 'Menton', and 'Elegant Lady' tulips (*Tulipa × 'Angélique', 'Menton', and 'Elegant Lady')—planted in groups under yarrow

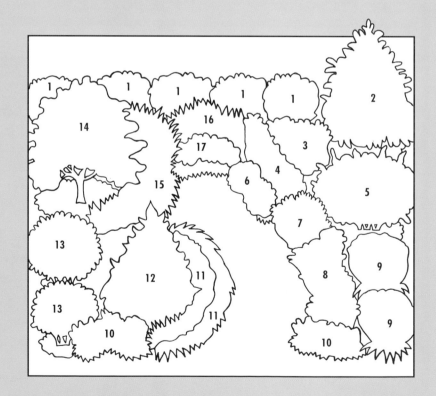

Garden for Deep Shade

Shade in the garden should be viewed not as a constraint but as an opportunity. It offers us a chance to create for ourselves a space evocative of all that is most appealing in a woodland setting. In the muted light of the shady garden we can appreciate the rich diversity of plant textures and forms, the great variations in shades of green, and the subtle beauty of woodland flowers. Here is the perfect setting for a garden that is both luxuriantly exuberant and dignified. If well planted and maintained, a garden in the shade has the power not only to delight our senses but to provide a respite from the glaring sun.

The main colors in this garden design are green and white. White is particularly useful in deep shade because it brightens even the darkest corner of the garden. Given the ephemeral nature of most perennial and shrub flowers, the emphasis in this garden is on foliage that can enliven the space over a long period of time. Several plants with green and white variegated leaves have thus been included, notably variegated Japanese iris, 'Sugar and Cream' hosta, variegated Japanese Solomon's seal, and a Mariesii hydrangea that sports a silvery white margin on the edge of its bright green foliage.

Different plants with burgundy- or mahogany-colored leaves are repeated throughout the garden as a unifying ele-

Lenten rose

ment. This color shows up quite well in the dim light of a shady garden, and many of these plants are evergreen (notably ajuga, epimedium, and the 'Olga Mezitt' rhododendron). Blue combines beautifully with this deep red foliage color, and is found in the flowers of plumbago, woodland phlox, ajuga, Arkansas amsonia, Japanese iris, scilla, and the Mariesii hydrangea (if it is planted in acidic soil), as well as in the chalky blue leaves of the 'Halcyon' and 'Krossa Regal' hostas.

The careful composition of different forms and textures is often what makes a garden truly exceptional. In this design, several coarse-leaved plants are positioned alongside finer-textured ones to create an aesthetically interesting picture throughout the growing season, whether or not the plants are flowering. One such example is the planting of bear's breeches, with its bold, sharply lobed foliage, right next to the delicately dissected leaves of astilbe. Irises are valuable because of their vertical form and because their narrow, elliptical leaves contrast so well with other plants. Japanese irises are particularly stately and elegant, and are more tolerant of shade than most other species of iris, as long as the soil stays evenly moist.

One of the more subtle ways in which a garden can mirror untamed nature is by changing with the seasons. There should always be something interesting to see in the garden, even in the dead of winter, and there should be something to which we can look forward. In this design, the winter landscape is brightened by the bell-shaped flowers of hellebores, masses of white snowdrops, and the warm burgundy foliage of ajuga, epimedium, and 'Olga Mezitt' rhododendron. In spring, blue and white flowers predominate, beginning with the sky blue flowers of the woodland phlox cultivar 'London Grove Blue' and the pure white flowers of Japanese pieris. The back wall will be illuminated in the spring by the bright white blossoms of the Japanese hydrangea vine, which puts on another impressive display in the autumn, when its leaves turn a golden yellow.

In summer the metallic blue leaves of the large hostas and the greens of many different ferns create a lush refuge. Masses of red and white astilbes light up the garden with great drama and remain attractive long after they have lost their vivid color. The hostas bloom and fill the air with their sweet fragrance. This is perhaps when the garden is most pleasurable, when you can sit with a book and enjoy the garden without feeling there are bothersome tasks to be completed.

The changes in the garden begin quietly enough as autumn approaches. The exotically elegant flowers of the toad-lily appear—these are fascinating when studied at close range. The blue flowers of plumbago are electrifying, especially when planted under the tea viburnum with its clusters of cherry red fruit. As the weather turns colder, the hostas mellow to a lovely clear yellow, and the golden color of Arkansas amsonia's needle-like leaves is downright breathtaking. Though the drama is over by Christmas, the garden remains attractive even at this rather bleak time, and before long the hellebores and snowdrops will be blooming again.

UNDERSTANDING THE NATURE OF SHADE

Variegated Solomon's seal

It is absolutely critical to understand the quantity and quality of light you have in your shady garden and how this light changes over time. The amount and duration of sunlight your garden receives will, to a great extent, determine the kinds of plants you can grow successfully. How does the light vary from season to season? What time of day do you have sunlight in the garden and is it direct or indirect light? What are your sources of shade? Most of us have a natural tendency to exaggerate the amount of sunlight our gardens receive (maybe it is wishful thinking), so before you spend a lot of time on an elaborate design, and certainly before you start planting, try to dispassionately analyze your specific situation.

Shade can generally be classed as partial, light, deep or full, and dense. If your site is sunny for a portion of the day, but is then shaded, you are working with partial shade. In lightly shady situations, the area is shaded for most or all of the day, but the shade is dappled. Deep shade is how we traditionally envision a shady garden—the area is consistently shaded throughout the day but the other growing conditions, such as soil and moisture, are good. In a densely shaded situation, the quality of light is the same as in a deeply shaded garden, but the other growing conditions are less than ideal. Tangled tree roots may prevent other plants from growing or the soil may be excessively soggy or dry. Once you've realistically assessed your site, you'll be able to choose a planting scheme well suited to the quality of light your garden receives.

Garden for Deep Shade
Plant List

1. Japanese hydrangea vine (*Schizophragma hydrangeoides*)
2. 'Mountain Fire' Japanese pieris (*Pieris japonica* 'Mountain Fire')
3. 'Halcyon' hosta (*Hosta* 'Halcyon')
4. 'Albo-Variegata' white-variegated hakone grass (*Hakonechloa macra* 'Albo-Variegata')
5. 'Deutschland' astilbe (*Astilbe* 'Deutschland')
6. 'White Towers' toad-lily (*Tricyrtis hirta* 'White Towers')
7. 'Purpurea crispa' dwarf bugle flower (*Ajuga pyramidalis* 'Purpurea crispa')
8. Variegated Japanese iris (*Iris ensata* 'Variegata')
9. Korean rock fern (*Polystichum tsus-simense*)
10. Barrenwort (*Epimedium rubrum*)
11. 'Olga Mezitt' rhododendron (*Rhododendron* 'Olga Mezitt')
12. Bear's breeches (*Acanthus mollis*)
13. Lenten rose (*Helleborus orientalis*)
14. Robust male ferns (*Dryopteris felix-mas undulata* 'Robusta')
15. 'Blue King' Japanese iris (*Iris ensata* 'Blue King')
16. Arkansas amsonia (*Amsonia hubrechtii*)
17. Tea viburnum (*Viburnum setigerum*)
18. 'Fanal' astilbe (*Astilbe* 'Fanal')
19. Plumbago (*Cerastostigma plumbaginoides*)
20. 'Jungle Beauty' large-leaved bugle flower (*Ajuga reptans* 'Jungle Beauty')
21. 'Sugar and Cream' hosta (*Hosta* 'Sugar and Cream')
22. 'London Grove Blue' woodland phlox (*Phlox divaricata* 'London Grove Blue')
23. Variegated Japanese Solomon's seal (*Polygonatum odoratum* var. *thunbergii* 'Variegatum')
24. 'Star at Midnight' Japanese iris (*Iris ensata* 'Star at Midnight')
25. 'Dora Amateis' rhododendron (*Rhododendron* 'Dora Amateis')
26. Soft shield fern (*Polystichum setiferum*)
27. Variegated Mariesii hydrangea (*Hydrangea macrophylla* 'Mariesii Variegata')
28. 'Krossa Regal' hosta (*Hosta* 'Krossa Regal')

Bulbs

Snowdrops (*Galanthus nivalis*)
'Spring Beauty' true scilla (*Scilla sibirica* 'Spring Beauty')
Windflower (*Anemone blanda*)

White Garden

To gardening devotees, the definitive white garden is at Sissinghurst Castle in Kent, England. Designed by Vita Sackville-West and her husband, Harold Nicolson, Sissinghurst's white garden is actually a subtle blend of white, silver, gray, and green. So many plants can be woven wonderfully into a white garden, combining interesting flowers and foliage, that selecting plants can be very difficult. Remember that a garden plan should serve only as a guideline waiting to be imprinted with each gardener's personality and style. In the words of Sackville-West, creating a garden with a single color theme is "great fun and endlessly amusing as an experiment, capable of perennial improvement, as you take away things that don't fit in and replace them by something you like better."

The white garden featured here centers on white and green—it offers a flush of soft white flowers in the spring, a steady display of various flowers in the summer, and a burst of starry, daisylike flowers in late summer and autumn. An underplanting of bulbs will give the garden an early start, and the dying foliage of the bulbs will be disguised by the foliage of later perennials. Structure is provided with a flagstone pathway interwoven with creeping white-flowered thyme, a white garden bench, and a clematis-covered arbor. Several tall, deep green

Sweet autumn clematis

arborvitae serve as a backdrop, accenting the white structures and flowers. While fragrance is not the focus of this garden, an observer seated on the garden bench may be teased by subtle scents that vary with the seasons.

Prepare the soil well before planting, adding compost and digging in shredded leaves to increase the organic matter in the soil. If the soil is very heavy clay or very compacted, you may want to add several yards of new topsoil, tilling it or (for lazier gardeners) just building a gentle berm above the existing soil. Good drainage is essential; consider creating an underground drainage system if water tends to sit in the planting area. Remove twine from balled and burlapped plants; you may also want to cut through the burlap and fold it back under the soil. Remove any plant ties or strings that the nursery may have left—these could cause problems if they are left on indefinitely. Under normal conditions it should not be necessary to stake any of the trees or shrubs. Plant them at the same level they were planted at the nursery; planting trees and shrubs too deeply can lead to future problems.

Use a starter fertilizer on the perennials and dig bone meal in with the bulbs. It is not necessary to use a starter fertilizer on trees. Instead, wait about a year—there is a danger that fertilizer

Snowy white tulips can begin the season in the white garden.

GARDENS WHILE YOU WAIT

Perennial gardens are not born overnight, however, it is possible to create an illusion of a well-established garden by selecting plants in one-gallon [3.8l] containers or larger and planting them closer together than normally recommended. As the plants become established, they can be divided to prevent overcrowding. Another option is to fill in bare spots with annuals until the perennials have increased in stature. White-flowering spider flowers (*Cleome hasslerana* 'Helen Campbell') can be used as an effective filler until the 'Snowbank' starflowers have reached their full height, and white-flowering morning glories will cover the arbor while the clematis becomes established.

Even when the perennials reach maturity, annuals can be useful to fill in bare spots that may occur—white impatiens or big-leaved white caladiums are perfect for a shady spot under a tree or shrub, while annual white vinca makes an excellent groundcover for a sunny spot. A grouping of containers or a single pot on a stone pedestal can become the garden's focal point while perennials are setting their roots. Fill two gray stone planters with double-flowered white petunias or daisy-shaped white zinnias, then edge the pots with silver licorice plant (*Helichrysum petiolare*) and sweet white alyssum (*Lobularia maritima* 'Carpet of Snow'). Set the planters opposite the garden bench and enjoy them all summer long. When the cooler weather arrives and the annuals start to drag, replace them with 'Illusion' or 'Encore' white chrysanthemums for a stunning autumn accent.

could damage the newly transplanted roots. Fertilize the perennials every two or three weeks, stopping in midsummer. Be careful not to overfertilize, or you will have beautiful foliage with few flowers. Roses, on the other hand, are heavy feeders that require plenty of food and water. The roses featured in this design are very hardy and do not require winter protection, deadheading, or special pruning (unless you want to improve the shape of the plant). The asters and coneflowers may bloom again later in the season if they are deadheaded early. The plumes of astilbes may be cut back once they have withered and the starflowers can be cut back once their bloom is finished; if you choose, both of these chores may be left until early spring. When the hostas finish flowering, dry flower stalks can be removed with a slight tug—the foliage should look good until early autumn. After the winter it may look as if the hostas have disappeared but the roots will still be thriving underground; watching the new shoots unfurl is one of the joys of spring.

Foamflower

Dusty miller

VARIATIONS ON A THEME

Plants with white flowers are easy to find, whether your garden is in sun, shade, or something in between. A white garden can focus on more than flowers, though—it can include silvery foliage plants, plants with "see-through" flowers, gray-leaved plants, and plants whose leaves are variegated white and green. Whites can be clear and bright, or they may be soft shades of ivory and cream.

Tall trees with silvery bark blend well in a white garden, while white-tipped conifers can carry the theme through winter months. In milder climates with soil on the acidic side, a woodland planting of white-flowering dogwoods, azaleas, and rhododendrons plus a 'Hally Jolivette' cherry offer a firm base for a springtime white garden. In somewhat cooler climates, an old-fashioned white garden for spring may be set around apple trees, white-flowering hybrid French lilacs, and peonies such as 'Festiva Maxima' or 'Krinkled White'.

Plants with silvery foliage tend to be sun-loving and drought-tolerant. The nonflowering form of lamb's ears (*Stachys byzantina* 'Silver Carpet') makes an excellent edger, as does the annual dusty miller (*Senecio cineraria*). Snow-in-summer (*Cerastium tomentosum*) forms dense, silvery mats that are covered in tiny white flowers from late spring into early summer. Many forms of wormwood (*Artemisia* spp.) create a subtle foil for white flowers, including the variety *Artemisia schmidtiana* 'Silver Mound'. Plants with "see-through" flowers include the misty plumes of baby's breath (*Gypsophilia paniculata* 'Bristol Fairy'), the tall clouds of colewort (*Crambe cordifolia*), and the glistening blades of silver reed grass (*Miscanthsis sinensis* 'Morning Light').

For a vertical aspect, add spiky plants such as delphinium, white veronica (*Veronica spicata* 'Icicle'), white lavender, white gayfeather (*Liatris scariosa* 'White Spires'), bugbane (*Cimicifuga racemosa*), and culver's root (*Veronicastrum virginicum* 'Album'). Other upright perennials include Jacob's ladder (*Polemonium caeruleum* 'Album'), white wild indigo (*Baptisia alba*), white Siberian iris (*Iris sibirica* 'King of Kings' or 'Fourfold White'), white valerian (*Centranthus ruber* 'Snowcloud'), white lily turf (*Liriope muscari* 'Monroe White'), bee balm (*Monarda didyma* 'Snow Queen'), and phlox (*Phlox paniculata* 'David').

Gardeners from every region, with every sort of weather and soil conditions, should be able to find plants in every size, shape, and color to create a unique white garden from groundcovers up to the tallest trees. Check on hardiness, ease of care, and availability while customizing your white garden. Plan first, then plant—and enjoy a garden brimming with lush foliage and delicate pale flowers of every form and habit.

White Garden Plant List

1. 'Emerald' arborvitae (*Thuja occidentalis* 'Emerald')
2. Sweet autumn clematis (*Clematis paniculata*)
3. 'Snow Queen' white clematis (*Clematis* × 'Snow Queen')
4. 'Blanc Double de Coubert' rose (*Rosa rugosa* 'Blanc Double de Coubert')
5. Compact Koreanspice viburnum (*Viburnum carlesii* 'Compacta')
6. 'Chanticleer' flowering pear (*Pyrus calleryana* 'Chanticleer')
7. 'Alba Meidiland' white groundcover roses (*Rosa* 'Alba Meidiland')
8. 'So Sweet' hosta (*Hosta* 'So Sweet')
9. Shadblow serviceberries (*Amelanchier canadensis*)
10. Foamflower (*Tiarella wherryi*)
11. 'Whirlwind' white fall anemone (*Anemone* × *hybrida* 'Whirlwind')
12. 'Crystal' white columbine (*Aquilegia* × 'Crystal')
13. 'Bridal Veil' white feather flower (*Astilbe* × *arendsii* 'Bridal Veil')
14. 'Grandiflora' hosta (*Hosta plantaginea* 'Grandiflora')
15. 'Album' white creeping thyme (*Thymus serpyllum* 'Album')
16. Whitefringe tree (*Chionanthus virginicus*)
17. 'Autumn Snow' New England aster (*Aster novae-angliae* 'Autumn Snow')
18. 'Snow Queen' oakleaf hydrangea (*Hydrangea quercifolia* 'Snow Queen')
19. 'White Swan' white-flowering purple coneflower (*Echinacea purpurea* 'White Swan')
20. 'Snowbank' starflower (*Boltonia asteroides* 'Snowbank')
21. 'SugarTyme' crab apple (*Malus* × 'SugarTyme')

Underplant with Bulbs to Extend the Bloom Season in Your Garden

'White Splendor' white windflowers (*Anemone blanda* 'White Splendor')—under serviceberries

'Album' pearls of Spain (*Muscari botryoides* 'Album')—under flowering pear tree

'Stainless' white daffodils (*Narcissus* × 'Stainless')—plant in clumps under crab apple tree

'Ice Wings' white daffodils (*Narcissus cyclamineus* 'Ice Wings')—plant in clumps under whitefringe tree

'Casa Blanca' white oriental lilies (*Lilium* × 'Casa Blanca')—under 'Grandiflora' hostas

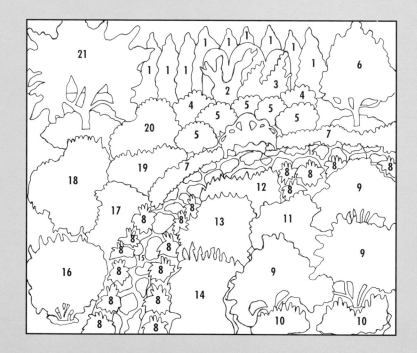

Raised Bed Herb Garden

Herbs seem especially well suited for containers and raised beds. Many, such as mint and tansy, are altogether too prolific to risk planting in an uncontained bed. Others, such as bee balm and salad burnet, self-seed with abandon and may crowd out less vigorous plants in a plant border. Window boxes and patio containers are ideal for culinary herbs that you may want to have in handy reaching distance from the kitchen. For more elaborate herb gardens, though, raised beds can be a practical idea.

The attraction of herbs can be for their culinary or medicinal value, for their fragrance, or for their flowers or form. Many herbs are used for dried flower arrangements or potpourris, or to prepare shampoos, soaps, and other beauty aids. Their needs are similar—most herbs perform best in sunny spots with well-drained soil that is not too heavy. The garden design for this raised bed herbal garden includes a selection of useful and ornamental plants, some of which provide structure and focal points, and others which provide color, fragrance, or interesting form. Several of the herbs featured—tarragon, rosemary, basil, and sage, in particular—have a variety of culinary uses.

There are two common forms of chamomile—Roman and German. Roman chamomile makes a fragrant groundcover but

'Dark Opal' purple basil

here I have included German chamomile, which is considered preferable for making tea. Pick the tiny flowers when the chamomile is in full bloom, and each time it flowers again. Spread out the flowers in a dry, shady spot to let them air dry for a few days—turn frequently and do not store until they have dried completely.

Some herbs, such as sage and basil, are available in so many colors, varieties, and forms that it would be possible to create an entire herb garden within a single genus of plants. In this garden design, I have restrained myself and included only culinary sage, but three forms of basil are featured. 'Dark Opal' is an award-winning cultivar that is an ornamental, aromatic form of sweet basil with dark purple leaves; it is often used to make colorful herb vinegar. Cinnamon basil is useful as an accent in fruit salads or meat marinades—be sure to use only fresh cinnamon basil, as the flavor dissipates when it is dried. Lemon basil is smaller and less vigorous than the other forms, with narrow, fragrant leaves and a mild flavor that is recommended for stir-fry recipes.

Lavender is one of the most useful herbs—it dries beautifully and makes wonderfully fragrant sachets and its fresh scent is often used in beauty products. It would be a must for any garden even without those added qualities, since its feathery foliage and purple spikes add form, color, and fragrance all summer long.

The problem with planting an herb garden—or designing one—is knowing when to quit. There are so many wonderful herbs readily available and reasonably priced that it is easy to become addicted. Follow the featured plan or substitute some of the herbs shown with your personal favorites. Don't be surprised if your herb garden expands into containers and window boxes—after all, they are beautiful, useful plants and there is always room for one more container.

Raised beds are perfect for growing herbs.

RAISED BEDS—THE ULTIMATE CONTAINER

Raised beds have all the benefits of container planting except portability. On the other hand, because of the size of most raised beds, they do not require the continual watering that most containers demand. The difficulty and expense of creating a raised bed vary depending on the depth of the bed and the materials used to build it. A shallow bed, 3 to 6 inches [7 to 15cm] deep, can be built fairly easily with pressure-treated wood, landscape timbers, railroad ties, or even recycled plastic "lumber" connectors and kits. Untreated redwood, cedar, hardwoods such as oak, or softer woods such as pine that have been pressure treated may be used for raised beds. Avoid timbers treated with creosote, pentachlorophenol, or CCA (chromium, copper, and arsenic compounds) since they contains toxins that can leach into the planting bed and can be inhaled when the wood is cut.

Shallow beds don't actually need to be retained at all—simply mound up the soil into a gently sloping berm and dig a spade edge to separate it from the lawn. Deeper beds—10 to 12 inches [25 to 30.5 cm]—are more suitable for growing root vegetables or where the bed is intended to replace poor soil. Deep beds can be made with the same materials mentioned above, but remember that the greater the depth of added soil, the greater the pressure on the sides of the bed—particularly when the soil is wet.

For sturdier raised beds, it can help to prepare a foundation or base of crushed gravel several inches deep, particularly when building a wall from flagstone or other flat stones. (Concrete blocks can be a less expensive alternative to stone walls.) Set the larger stones at the base and stagger the stones so that they create an overlapping pattern. Fill in gaps with topsoil or gravel as you build up each level. Pockets of topsoil between the rocks can be planted with moss, creeping thyme, sedum varieties such as 'Dragon's Blood', or other tiny-leaved, creeping plants.

While raised beds can vary dramatically in form and design, even the most basic designs can solve many landscape problems.

DRAINAGE

Very few plants like "wet feet"—roots sitting in water—and, particularly in the winter time, many plants will not survive this condition. It may be possible to improve drainage with soil amendments or to install an underground drainage system to alleviate the problem of water sitting on top of the soil. Raised beds offer a solution to drainage problems by raising the soil above ground level—anywhere from a few inches up to about a foot [7 to 30cm]. (Soil can be built up even higher, but because of the pressure exerted on the framework, anything built up more than a foot or so will need something sturdier than a raised bed to contain it—more on the lines of a retaining wall.)

SOIL PROBLEM SOLVER

Poor soil, heavily compacted soil, or heavy clay soil are not conducive to healthy plant growth. A raised bed can help solve this problem, since all new soil can be added to fill the bed. Some topsoil suppliers will sell compost or shredded leaves (if you don't have your own) that can be mixed with the topsoil before installing it. Customize the soil to suit the plants you will be adding—mix in sand for plants that prefer a lighter soil or amendments such as peat for acid-loving plants. Soil in a raised bed should periodically be replaced or topped up with "fresh" topsoil to keep it from getting "stale."

EASY ACCESS

For gardeners in wheelchairs or those with aching backs and joints, raised beds can be a blessing. Long, narrow beds raised a foot above the ground can make gardening posssible from a wheelchair with careful planning—making sure to create wide, level paths between the beds. If the raised bed is going to be shallow,

lay black weed-preventing fabric over the ground before adding the new topsoil. Even with a deeper bed, this will discourage turf and weeds from coming up. It is also easier on the back than digging out existing turf and weeds first. The sides of raised beds made with flagstones or other wide, flat stones on a sturdy base can double as seats. Seats can also be added to wooden raised beds by securing 2" x 6" [5 to 15cm] pieces of lumber along the top edge. Cover the bed with a three-inch (7cm) layer of finely shredded mulch for weed control, and you have created a very low-maintenance planting area.

Borage

RAISED BED HERB GARDEN PLANT LIST

1. 'Berggarten' culinary sage, (*Salvia officinalis* 'Berggarten')
2. 'Munstead' lavender (*Lavandula angustifolia* 'Munstead')
3. 'Conica' dwarf Alberta spruce (*Picea glauca* 'Conica')
4. 'Pink Color Up' ornamental cabbage (*Brassica oleracea* 'Pink Color Up')
5a. 'Dark Opal' basil (*Ocimum basilicum* 'Dark Opal')
5b. Cinnamon basil (*Ocimum basilicum* 'Cinnamon')
5c. Lemon basil (*Ocimum basilicum* var. *citriodorum*)
6. True French tarragon (*Artemisia dranunculus*)
7. Rosemary (*Rosmarinus officinalis*)
8. 'The Fairy' standard form rose (*Rosa* × 'The Fairy')
9. Creeping red thyme (*Thymus serpyllum* 'Coccineus')
10. German chamomile (*Matricaria recutita*)

Antique Rose and Heirloom Flower Garden

Much of what we love about gardening is based on nostalgia, so it is no surprise that we long to re-create flower gardens out of the idyllic past. Flowers from our childhood memories or from the reminiscences of our parents and grandparents have special meaning for us, and if flowers are entwined with thoughts of family and friends, those blooms will eventually work their way into our gardens. There must be some rhyme or reason for this phenomenon—we don't know why it happens, we just know that it does.

I almost talked my husband into buying a small house in England before we ever saw the inside or asked the price, simply because of the huge display of single hollyhocks rising above the backyard fence. As a child, my small garden consisted of marigolds, zinnias, snapdragons, four o'clocks, and morning glories—plants that have somehow worked their way into every single garden I have planted ever since. My ninety-two-year-old grandmother still refers to the house where she lived in Louisville sixty years ago as the one with "that beautiful redbud tree." Our garden memories link us to our past through the gardens we plant today.

The roses featured in the accompanying plan are antique but not ancient: the hybrid perpetual 'Reine des Violettes', a heavy repeat bloomer, was developed in 1860. 'Belle de Crécy' is a very fragrant gallica rose dating back to at least the early part of the nineteenth century. The alba rose 'Konigin von Danemarck', which features scarlet hips all winter, was introduced in 1826. 'Madame Hardy' is a damask rose dating back to 1832, with lemon fragrance and double flowers that bloom in clusters. Because roses grow best without too much root competition, the accompanying plan positions the roses against an open trellis backdrop, with the delicate, self-seeding annual flowers of love-in-a-mist to set them off. The modern cultivar 'Persian Jewels' is used instead of the species simply because it is more readily available.

Spider flower, hyacinth bean, and globe amaranth are also annuals, while sweet William is a biennial. Reseed the area where sweet William is planted each year to ensure flowering from year to year. Purple coneflower is a drought-resistant native flower that holds up well, but the tall mallow 'Zebrina' may need to be replaced after a harsh winter. Globe amaranth holds up exceptionally well to heat and drought—it does fill in quite well, but I like to plant it fairly close together to ensure a solid mass of flowers. Love-in-a-mist and hyacinth bean will grow rapidly from seed that has been sown directly into the soil when

'Konigin von Danemarck'

the danger of frost is past. Spider flower and globe amaranth will be more effective if you can find a source that sells them by the flat. The newer cultivar of globe amaranth called 'Lavender Lady' performs exceptionally well and blooms from late spring to late autumn.

Whether you choose to seek out the seeds of original heirloom plants or to grow their twentieth-century offspring (or even if you prefer the improved hybrids or cultivars of the heirloom plants), you will be making a connection with the past. It's always interesting to find out how and when your favorite flowers first appeared, especially if the scene was set in the distant past. The hunt for antique roses is a hobby for the easily obsessed, and it can take you across the country or across the globe. Rose rustlers, in the best sense of the word, are out to salvage old roses from neglected roadsides and deserted farmhouses. Others spend their time tracing the genealogy of different roses to track down and identify their distant ancestors genetically.

In a society addicted to disposables, it's nice to know that some things are made to last.

FLOWERS FROM YEARS PAST

Most of the plants featured in the accompanying plan date back at least as far as Colonial times, and some even to ancient times. Old books, letters, and garden plans are often the source of our information about these plants of the past. In Harper & Brothers' *Fifth Reader of the School and Family Series*, published in 1861, more than a quarter of the book is devoted to the study of botany (liberally peppered with illustrations and romantic garden verse).

Plants listed in the rose family at that time included damask rose, moss rose, cinnamon rose, wild-pine strawberry, and several species of what were then called spirea. Listed in the "camellia, mallow, and citron families" were Japanese camellias, hollyhocks, musk mallows, lemon, lime, orange, and others. The lesson featuring "Leguminous and Umbelliferous Plants" included wild lupine, mimosa, upright indigo, wild carrot, and poison hemlock. The composite (sunflower) family listed Chinese chrysanthemum, many-flowered sunflower, China aster, wild dahlia, and French marigold, while the "Jessamine, Honeysuckle, and Heath" family included woodbine honeysuckle, trumpet honeysuckle, and several types of jasmine. Still others were listed with the "Labiate and Trumpet-Flower" families: California trumpet flower (*Chelone centranthifolia*), scarlet salvia, French lavender, and garden thyme.

In addition to old books about flowers and new books about old flowers, look to the gardens at Monticello and other restored gardens of the past for records of the flowers that were originally grown there. Some of the plants may be hard to find today, but a surprising number are readily available (although possibly only in seed form).

Sweet William

Tall mallow

ANTIQUE ROSE AND HEIRLOOM FLOWER GARDEN PLANT LIST

1. Hyacinth bean (*Dolichos lablab*)—seeds sown directly into the soil at intervals along the free-standing trellised fence (after danger of frost)
2. Spider flower (*Cleome hasslerana*, mixed colors) (Start indoors from seed and transplant after danger of frost if flats or plant plugs are not available.)
3. 'Madame Hardy' damask rose (*Rosa damascena* 'Madame Hardy')
4. 'Konigin von Danemarck' alba rose (*Rosa alba* 'Konigin von Danemarck')
5. 'Belle de Crécy' gallica rose (*Rosa gallica* 'Belle de Crécy')
6. 'Reine des Violettes' hybrid perpetual rose (*Rosa* 'Reine des Violettes')
7. Purple coneflower (*Echinacea purpurea*)
8. 'Zebrina' tall mallow (*Malva sylvestris* 'Zebrina')
9. Sweet William (*Dianthus barbatus*)
10. Globe amaranth (*Gomphrena globosa*, mixed colors)
11. 'Persian Jewels' love-in-a-mist (*Nigella damascena* 'Persian Jewels')

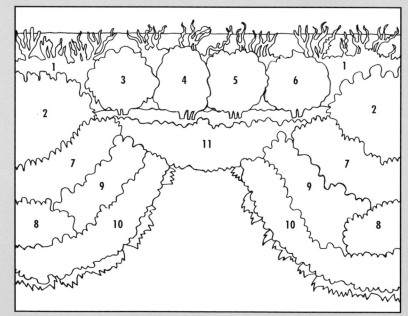

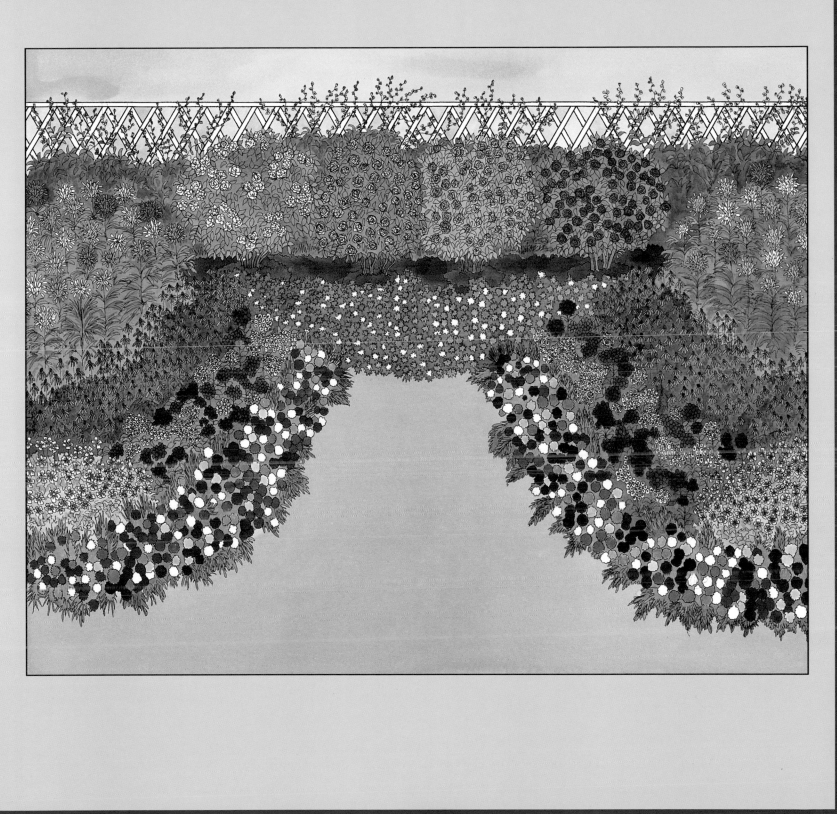

Medieval Pleasure Garden

From the Garden of Eden and on through time, gardens have played an important part in the history of mankind. Then, as now, gardens served many purposes and came in many forms. The legendary hanging gardens of Babylon, one of the seven wonders of the ancient world, were said to be a series of terraced gardens constructed of glazed brick and arranged in five tiers connected by a winding staircase and each level rising about fifty feet (15m) above the last. Fountains irrigated exotic plants in the "hanging" gardens through an elaborate pumping system—all this five hundred years before the birth of Christ.

While interest in gardening waxed and waned over the years, ancient societies were always dependent on culinary herbs, crop plants, and medicinal plants. The ornamental features of plants were often considered negligible in relationship to other, more practical uses. During medieval times gardening was present as ever, but gardening plans and practices went largely unrecorded. What little record we have of medieval gardens comes from historical detective work, and most of it relates to English gardens.

By examining paintings of the period, illustrations of medieval gardens can be found—unfortunately, depicting detailed background landscapes in paintings did not become common until the latter part of the medieval period. The writings of Geoffrey Chaucer (1340–1400) and other medieval poetry occasionally show us glimpses of the flowers and gardens of the times but, again, most of these were written toward the end of the period. Archaeological researchers in England believe they have uncovered traces of medieval gardens but accurate, detailed information is hard to come by.

English society in the Middle Ages was in no way democratic. Royalty and the landed gentry were wealthy beyond belief, with elaborate gardens and huge parks making up hundreds of acres, sometimes featuring "menageries" similar to the zoos or wildlife parks of today. Middle-class citizens, owners of moderate-size town homes or country manor houses on several acres, might have an orchard as well as an herb garden. Farmers, merchants, and the more prosperous peasants would have to settle for an "herber"—a small ornamental garden—of an acre or less on their modest cottage lots.

Since most of us poor folk today are gardening in relatively small spaces, the latter type of medieval garden is the most practical to re-create. An herber was a type of "pleasure garden," not intended for food, although it commonly featured culinary herbs and medicinal plants as well as ornamental flowers. While

Red Rose of Lancaster

larger medieval gardens were in parklike settings, herbers were likely to include lawn, herbaceous gardens, water features, seating areas, and walled enclosures.

Turf was carefully tended and scythed to create a lawn like "green velvet," and sections of lawn were outlined by walks and narrow herbaceous beds, often accompanied by tunnels of trees and roses or by arbors covered with climbing vines or roses. Where the turf was laid flush with the herbaceous beds, the beds were usually slightly raised and separated from the turf by stone, brick, or timber. Where dirt, sand, stone, or gravel walks separated the turf from the beds, the beds were often left flush with the walk. Benches, usually backless, were a common feature—either made of stone or timbers and often topped with turf seats. Benches were often built in a semicircular pattern called an exedra so that visitors to the garden could sit and socialize in comfort.

In her book *The Medieval Garden* Sylvia Landsberg quotes a work by Albertus Magnus, a thirteenth-century Dominican churchman who described the ideal layout of an herber in some detail:

> *Care must be taken that the lawn is of such a size that it may be planted with every sweet-smelling herb such as rue and sage and basil, and likewise all sorts of flowers, as violet, columbine, lily, rose, iris and the like. Between these herbs and the turf, at the edge of the lawn, set square, let there be a higher bench of turf, flowering and lovely; and somewhere in the middle provide seats....Behind the lawn there may be a great diversity of medicinal and scented herbs....There should not be any trees in the middle of the lawn, but let its surface delight in the open air....If possible a clean fountain of water in a stone basin should be in the midst.*

The structure of such a small pleasure garden can vary greatly in cost, depending on the materials used, while still following the pattern of a true medieval herber. If you have skills with adobe or with brick, construct the walls of your enclosed garden out of these materials, topping the walls with a crenellated pattern like those of a medieval castle. Hedgerows were common enclosures, but the art of creating a hedgerow—as opposed to a simple hedge—never seemed to reach North America, and besides, the sweetbriar rose—which was usually combined with hawthorn and honeysuckle to form the hedgerow—is not hardy throughout much of the United States and Canada.

A medieval fence enclosure would be easier to re-create—these included split-oak lath trellis fences, square- or diamond-patterned pole fences, and wattle, palisade, or close-board sawn fences. A basic walk can be created with gravel on a bed of sand, or you can eliminate the walkways altogether by extending the turf to the edge of the herbaceous border and raising the level of the planting bed.

If you are an obsessive type and you want a really accurate medieval garden, seek out the few available books on the subject and research the period through the art, literature, architecture, and political records of the times. The accompanying garden plan follows the general outline of a medieval herber, with concessions to modern budgets, lot sizes, and plant availability. The herbaceous beds contain a mixture of medicinal, aromatic, and mainly ornamental flowers—modify the suggested plantings to your heart's content. The purpose of a medieval pleasure garden, after all, was mainly to bring delight to its beholder—and would you really want a peacock in the backyard?

MEDIEVAL PLANTS

To find the plants that grew in medieval gardens, read the verses of Chaucer and other writers of the period. The difficulty is that many of the plants were called by different names or that they have evolved almost beyond recognition over the years. Of the medieval plants known today, herbs may be the closest to their original form. Many of the roses found in medieval gardens are still available today but not all species of the ancient roses will survive on the North American continent.

As listed in poems and other literature of the times, popular plants included iris, columbine, lily-of-the-valley, peony, fern, cornflower, red corn poppy, periwinkle, ox-eye daisies, yellow corn marigold, borage, chamomile, wild strawberries, hyssop, parsley, lily, avens (geum), betony, rue, hollyhock, sage, violet, woodbine, wild thyme, ginger, carnations or pinks, colewort, leek, cinnamon, speedwell, honeysuckle, marguerites, pansies, sweet basil, dill, marjoram, rosemary, sweet woodruff, roses, and daisies (or "day's eyes").

Chaucer mentions "pillar elm," "builder oak," "hardy ash," "boxtree" (boxwood), maple, palm, laurel, and yew; other trees and shrubs mentioned by other medieval authors include quince, wild plum, fig, date, pear, nutmeg, olive, peach, medlar, service (serviceberry), "chesteynes" (chestnut), hazel, willow, apple, crab apple, cherry, pine, cypress, filbert, fir, juniper, almond, hawthorn, poplar, linden and St. John's wort.

Roses available at the time included the Red Rose of Lancaster, *Rosa gallica* 'Officinalis'; the White Rose of York, *Rosa alba* 'Semi-Plena'; the damask rose, *Rosa damascena*; the Austrian Copper rose, *Rosa foetida* 'Bicolor'; and the Eglantine or Shakespeare rose, *Rosa rubiginosa*.

While many of the herbaceous perennials of medieval times are still around, unless you are a real stickler for accuracy the newer cultivars may be preferable for their improved hardiness and disease-resistance. Some, like the peony, are widely available in newer, named cultivars but almost impossible to find in species form. The accompanying garden plan includes modern cultivars of some antique plants for the reasons mentioned above. Also, please note that while the cockspur hawthorn has good autumn color and is truer to the medieval period, the thornless cockspur hawthorn is much safer to use where children will be present.

MEDIEVAL PLEASURE GARDEN PLANT LIST

1. 'Greenspire' littleleaf linden (*Tilia cordata* 'Greenspire')
2. Red Rose of Lancaster (*Rosa gallica* 'Officinalis')
3. White Rose of York (*Rosa alba* 'Semi-Plena')
4. Thornless cockspur hawthorn (*Craetagus crus-galli* var. *inermis*)
5. Lady fern (*Athyrium felix-femina*)
6. Lily-of-the-valley (*Convallaria majalis*)
7. 'East Coast Hybrids' single hollyhocks (*Alcea rosea*)
8. 'Moonlight' hardy marguerites (*Anthemis tinctoria* 'Moonlight')
9. Fernleaf dill (*Anethum graveolens*)
10. Cornflower (*Centaurea montana*)
11. 'Becky' hybrid shasta daisy (*Leucanthemum* × 'Becky')
12. Sweet basil (*Ocimum basilicum*)
13. Madonna lily (*Lilium candidum*)
14. 'Blue Charm' speedwell (*Veronica spicata* 'Blue Charm')
15. 'Warlock' poppy (*Papaver orientale* 'Warlock')
16. Culinary sage (*Salvia officinalis*)
17. Compact thyme (*Thymus* × 'Compactus')

Garden Rockery

An alpine garden might also be a rock garden, but a rockery is not necessarily a garden of "alpines." The accompanying garden plan features a selection of low-growing, creeping, crawling, or neatly mound-shaped plants with diminutive proportions suitable for a rockery. These plants do not all fall under the description of "alpines," but all work well in the company of rocks.

If you need a pickaxe to break into your stony soil, forget the manmade nature of the rockery as shown and scratch a similar planting area directly out of your landscape. Select a sunny spot where the rocks are set in a staggered pattern on a slope or outcropping. Work a mixture of sand, peat, and topsoil (plus compost, if you have it) into the crevices between the rocks and use each pocket of this planting mix as a miniature planting bed. After planting, spread a few handfuls of mulch around each new transplant and water it in well. (Be careful not to flood it, though, or the soil might wash away.)

In a narrow city lot or confined condominium garden, try adapting the accompanying plan into a steeper rockery—building up instead of across to reduce the amount of land required for the garden. Set staggered rocks against a brick or concrete wall (a wooden structure will rot) and pack them together tightly with a planting mix as described above. Make sure the slope is not excessively tall or steeply inclined—visitors to your garden should be breathless with appreciation, not fear of a landslide. For best results, consult a landscape architect to ensure that the rock wall will be stable, secure, and built to last.

The rockery, as shown, consists of a gently sloping berm rising to about eighteen inches (45cm) above the ground. When installing the topsoil/peat/sand/compost mix to create the berm, work in rocks of similar color but assorted shapes and sizes, "holey boulders" with pockets that can be filled with soil, and a few flat, wide stone slabs in a balanced, random pattern. What nature doesn't provide, we have to play around with a little—the effect should be unstructured and as natural as possible. A rough edging of rocks could be used to separate the rockery from adjacent turf, or a gravel walk (set on a sand base) could be installed alongside the berm.

Once the framework of the rockery is either installed or created out of the natural landscape, it is time to consider the plants that will inhabit this small ecosystem. Traditionally, rock

Dalmatian bellflower

and alpine gardens are set in sunny locations with plants that, apart from occasional taller accents, stay under a foot tall. A rockery in a partly shaded spot could house small ferns, tiny hostas, primulas, and prostrate evergreens; in moist shade, garden moss (*Sphagnum recurvum* or *S. papillosum*) or mossy, spreading pearlwort (*Sagina subulata*) could be included.

For a sunny rockery, consider compact plants that might not usually be considered for a rockery—any of the newer, compact daylilies, for instance, or low-growing grasses that will not spread out of bounds. Fill in bare spots with little annuals, cactus, or succulents—in most regions, these will not last the winter but they can still be effective until frost. Don't be afraid to experiment and try something new—what's the worst that can happen? If a single plant dies—as some are bound to—it's not a major loss, and if it doesn't look right you can either give it away or throw it away. On the other hand, you may find a treasure that will one day hold pride of place in the rockery.

Many plants will thrive in the soil pockets between rocks.

Sensational Spring-Flowering Selections

Virtually any rockery can be planted to include a burst of spring bloom by under- (or inter-) planting small bulbs with later-blooming plants. Combine the bulbs with the mossy foliage and mat-forming pastel colors of creeping phlox (*Phlox subulata*) for a bolder effect. The following bulbs should be readily available from mail order nurseries if not always at local garden centers:

CROCUS (MOST FOUR TO SIX INCHES [10 TO 15CM] TALL)

'Blue Bird' (*Crocus chrysanthus* 'Blue Bird')—Deep violet with inner white petals

'Advance' (*Crocus chrysanthus* 'Advance')—Purple shades with yellow inside

'Cream Beauty' (*Crocus chrysanthus* 'Cream Beauty')—Creamy white

'Snow Bunting' (*Crocus chrysanthus* 'Snow Bunting')—White touched with lavender

DAFFODIL (MOST EIGHT TO TEN INCHES [20 TO 25CM] TALL)

'Surfside' (*Narcissus* × 'Surfside')—White petals with creamier trumpet

'February Gold' Cyclamineus Hybrid Narcissus (*Narcissus* × 'February Gold')—Good yellow color

'Hawera' Triandrus Hybrid Narcissus (*Narcissus* × 'Hawera')—Lemon yellow flower

Petticoat Narcissus (*Narcissus bulbocodium*)—Yellow/orange cupped flowers

'Tête-á-Tête' Cyclamineus Hybrid Narcissus (*Narcissus* × 'Tête-á-Tête')—Lemon yellow

GLORY-OF-THE-SNOW

Glory-of-the-snow (*Chionodoxa luciliae*)—Brilliant blue flowers, only five to ten inches (12 to 25cm) high; also available in white and pink varieties

GRAPE HYACINTH

'Blue Spike' (*Muscari armeniacum* 'Blue Spike')—Double-flowered form of the species

'Album' (*Muscari azureum* 'Album')—White-flowering form

HYACINTH (MOST EIGHT TO TEN INCHES [20 TO 25CM] TALL)

'Jan Bos' (*Hyacinthus* × 'Jan Bos')—Scarlet red

'White Pearl' (*Hyacinthus* × 'White Pearl')—Pure white

'City of Haarlem' (*Hyacinthus* × 'City of Haarlem')—Deep yellow

'Gypsy Queen' (*Hyacinthus* × 'Gypsy Queen')—Apricot

'Champagne' (*Hyacinthus* × 'Champagne')—White flushed with pink

'Blue Surprise' (*Hyacinthus* × 'Blue Surprise')—Deep blue flowers

IRIS

Dwarf iris (*Iris reticulata*)—Yellow/orange, white, blue, and violet flowers

TULIP

'Plaisir' (*Tulipa greigii* 'Plaisir')—eight to twelve inches (20 to 30cm) tall, cream flowers stroked with bright red

'Heart's Delight' (*Tulipa kaufmanniana* 'Heart's Delight')—six to nine inches (15 to 23cm) tall, red petals edged with pink and accented with yellow

'Lilac Wonder' (*Tulipa bakeri* 'Lilac Wonder')—eight inches (20cm) tall, pink with yellow center, resembling a crocus

'Bright Gem' (*Tulipa batalinii* 'Bright Gem')—six inches (15cm) tall, pale yellow

'Persian Pearl' (*Tulipa pulchella* 'Persian Pearl')—Only three to four inches (7 to 10cm) tall, deep wine red flowers with yellow centers

WINDFLOWER

Mixed-color windflowers (*Anemone blanda*)—White, pink, lilac, magenta, and purple daisy-like flowers that seem to vanish after flowering, four to six inches (10 to 15cm) tall

GARDEN ROCKERY PLANT LIST

1. Yellow stonecrop (*Sedum kamtschaticum*)
2. 'Silver Mound' artemisia (*Artemisia schmidtiana* 'Silver Mound')
3. 'Resholt' Dalmatian bellflower (*Campanula portenschlagiana* 'Resholt')
4. 'Snowstorm' coral bells (*Heuchera sanguinea* 'Snowstorm')
5. 'Dragon's Blood' stonecrop (*Sedum spurium* 'Dragon's Blood')
6. Cushion spurge (*Euphorbia polychroma*)
7. Golden-edge lemon thyme (*Thymus × citriodorus* 'Aureus')
8. 'Dusseldorf Pride' sea thrift (*Armeria maritima* 'Dusseldorf Pride')
9. 'China Doll' Carpathian harebell (*Campanula carpatica* 'China Doll')
10. Hardy ice plant (*Delosperma cooperi*)
11. 'Tiny Rubies' cheddar pinks (*Dianthus gratianopolitanus* 'Tiny Rubies')
12. 'Nana Gracilis' false cypress (*Chamaecyparis obtusa* 'Nana Gracilis')
13. 'Mother Lode' prostrate juniper (*Juniperus horizontalis* 'Mother Lode')
14. Pink tickseed (*Coreopsis rosea*)
15. Golden barberry (*Berberis thunbergii* 'Aurea')
16. 'Blue Star' singleseed juniper (*Juniperus squamata* 'Blue Star')

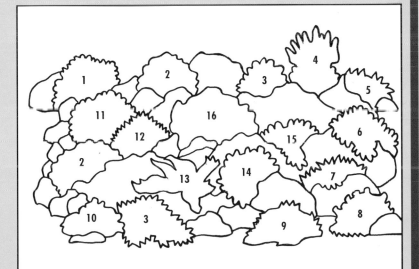

Two Cutting Gardens:
For Sun and Shade

Cutting gardens are designed to supply the gardener with an abundance of flowers and seedheads to use indoors, primarily in decorative arrangements. If space allowed, a garden consisting solely of flowers suitable for cutting would be ideal. Most of us, however, do not have the expanse of land to justify such exclusivity. Nor do we have the time to devote to creating and maintaining yet another garden, distinct from the spaces in which we already have plants growing. This plan solves the problem by integrating a cutting garden into an area where almost everyone already has at least a few ornamental plants growing, namely the foundation of the house.

Foundation plantings are notoriously dull. An azalea here and there (usually one that will be excessively large within a few years), maybe a conifer or two. In this design, on the other hand, plants with flowers for cutting become an integral part of the foundation planting. Not only does this enliven a prominent area, it also places the flowers to be cut in a highly accessible location.

This design recognizes, furthermore, that not all plants with flowers good for cutting are grown in full sun. Our image of "a cutting garden" may be of sunflowers, cosmos, lilies, and other sun-lovers, but there are shade-loving plants with beautiful flowers for cutting as well. To give a complete picture there are two separate plans: a single yard features both full-sun plantings and shade plants.

Several different woody plants are included, both deciduous and evergreen, to give the garden a persistent structure and form. Placed right alongside the path, where its fragrant blossoms can be appreciated up close, is a mildew-resistant lilac called Preston hybrid lilac. It is extremely free-flowering and excellent for cutting. Also in the sunny area are three 'William Penn' barberries. They are dense and compact, growing only four feet (1.2m) tall at maturity, and are attractive throughout the year. In summer the leaves are a glossy bright green and in winter they turn a glowing purplish burgundy. The cheerful yellow flowers are not appropriate for cutting but are lovely nonetheless.

A small cultivar of crab apple known as 'Jewelberry' assumes a prominent place in the corner of the foundation planting, effectively anchoring the garden. Cut a few branches in late winter and force the flowers to open indoors. As showy as the flowers are in spring, white with a delicate blush of pink, the fruit of this cultivar from late summer through early winter is just as glorious and splendid in arrangements. 'Jewelberry' bears

Love-in-a-mist

clusters of bright, cherry red fruit that are truly a stunning sight on a gray, wintry day.

A cutting garden without roses is almost unimaginable. Hybrid tea roses are demanding of time and attention, however, and are chemically dependent despite our best intentions. The rose used here is a hybrid rugosa rose, and is remarkably tough and disease-resistant. This cultivar, called 'Frau Dagmar Hartopp', has single, silvery pink flowers in great profusion beginning in spring. The flowers have an intriguing clove scent and are followed in autumn by bright red hips. Unlike the constant care demanded by hybrid teas, this stalwart rugosa needs only to have its old, worn out canes removed each year. Prune these out in late winter or early spring to maintain vigor and ensure good air circulation.

The Burkwood viburnum cultivar known as 'Conoy' is a relatively recent introduction and ideal where space is limited. Its dark red flower buds appear in early spring, opening in April or May to fragrant white flower clusters. Prune off a few stems in late winter or very early spring to force inside. Even just one stem in a bud vase can lift your spirits until spring truly arrives. The leaves of this cultivar are a deep, shiny green, and far more attractive than the foliage of most other evergreen viburnums. In late summer and autumn the glossy leaves are complemented by brilliant red, fairly persistent fruit.

The woody plants selected for the shady side of the garden also have flowers or fruit useful for arrangements. The inkberry

Oakleaf hydrangea

cultivar called 'Leucocarpa' has unusual, bright white fruit. A cultivar of oakleaf hydrangea known as 'Snow Queen' has massive white conical trusses beginning in late summer. The flowers start out pure white and gradually change over time to pale pink. They are dramatic in a bowl or vase and can be used either fresh or dried. The huge, textured leaves turn a dazzling burgundy color in autumn and are also outstanding in arrangements.

A determined effort has been made in recent years to develop cold-hardy camellias for all of those northerners who lusted for so long after the exquisite flowers they saw in autumn and winter in gardens further south. The camellia used here is one of the hardiest, reportedly to -12°F (-11°C). The vivid white flowers start to bloom in autumn and look very much like peonies. These lush, profuse blooms are absolutely striking when set on a table in a glass bowl.

A notable facet of this particular design is that there is something interesting to cut and bring indoors throughout the year. In winter the elegant flowers of Christmas roses are charming in a vase, as are the cut branches of spring-blooming woody plants. By April and May you can cut such diverse treasures as peony, crab apple, lilac, and viburnum flowers, the fragrant deep blue spikes of lavender, stately Japanese iris blossoms, and the curious blooms of a cultivar of masterwort known as 'Shaggy', to name just a few. In summer this garden is exceedingly lush and exuberant. Roses,

larkspur, false sunflower, summer phlox, lilies, Russian sage, and baby's breath, among other plants, are in full bloom in the sunny garden. In the shade the different astilbes flower in breathtaking shades of peach, pink, and red; the ferns are a deep, rich green; the golden yellow flower spikes of ragwort are compelling against midnight black stems; and the sweet scent of hosta flowers perfumes the air.

By late summer and autumn the ornamental grasses have bloomed and are starting to set seed. The inflorescences of these particular grasses are superb in arrangements, adding a color and texture not typically found in cut flowers. The gracefully arching spikelets of Northern sea oats are especially notable, for they will, if cut in the summer, hold onto their luminescent green color even after being brought indoors. They are charming when combined in a vase with the autumn flowers of aster, boltonia, montbretia, monkshood, and oakleaf hydrangea.

A cutting garden need not be an isolated patch that flowers exclusively in full sun in the depths of summer's heat. It should be accessible and attractive all year round and limited only by your budget and imagination.

HANDLING CUT FLOWERS

The flowers you cut and bring inside from the garden will last longer if you follow a few common-sense rules:

- The best time to cut flowers is early in the morning, when the temperature is coolest and before the morning dew evaporates.

- Make a clean cut with a sharp pruning shears or scissors. Cut the flowers at an angle and if the stems are particularly thick or woody make a one- to two-inch (2.5 to 5cm) cut from the base of the stem upwards to facilitate water absorption.

- Try to pick your flowers when they are at just the right stage for cutting. If cut when the buds are tightly closed they are unlikely ever to open. If the flowers you cut are at the very peak of their bloom, on the other hand, they will probably not last too much longer when brought inside. Pick flowers that bloom in clusters when roughly half of the blooms are open.

- Try to carry the flower stems with their heads down to keep the stems straight and to keep the flower heads from breaking.

- Once inside, cut stems at an angle again and put them as soon as possible in a bucket of lukewarm water.

- Put the bucket in a cool spot out of direct sunlight and leave it until the water reaches room temperature. For best results let the flowers sit in this position overnight, or at the least for a few hours.

- If the flowers you cut have a hollow stem—poppies, Mexican sunflowers, and dahlias for example—you must sear the end of the stem right after cutting. This is also true for plants that secrete a milky substance, such as euphorbia and milkweed. Only after the stem ends of such plants have been seared with a candle or over a burner should they be put in the bucket of tepid water.

- Roses and tulips tend to open very quickly once picked. You can slow this process by carefully holding the blooms closed with florist's tape until you are ready to display the flowers.

- The container you use for your arrangement should be thoroughly clean, and any leaves that would be under water must be removed.

- Remove the pollen-bearing stems of each bloom when using lilies to avoid having the stamens fall off and stain whatever surface your arrangement is sitting on.

- Your cut flowers will last longer if placed out of direct sunlight and temperature extremes and far from the drying winds of fans or air conditioners.

Properly conditioning cut flowers will extend their vase life.

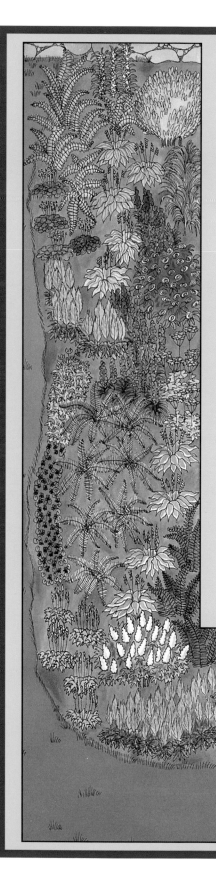

SHADY CUTTING GARDEN PLANT LIST

1. 'Blue King' iris (*Iris ensata* 'Blue King')
2. 'Red Light' astilbe (*Astilbe* 'Red Light')
3. 'Dorothy Wycoff' Japanese pieris (*Pieris japonica* 'Dorothy Wycoff')
4. 'Bressingham Bronze' alumroot (*Heuchera micrantha* 'Bressingham Bronze')
5. 'Blue Moon' hosta (*Hosta* 'Blue Moon')
6. 'Shaggy' masterwort (*Astrantia major* ssp. *involucrata* 'Shaggy')
7. 'Hewitt's Double' meadow rue (*Thalictrum delvayi* 'Hewitt's Double')
8. Wallich's wood fern (*Dryopteris wallichiana*)
9. 'Elizabeth Bloom' astilbe (*Astilbe* 'Elizabeth Bloom')
10. 'Snow Queen' oakleaf hydrangea (*Hydrangea quercifolia* 'Snow Queen')
11. 'Snow White' heucherella (*Heucherella tiarelloides* 'Snow White')
12. 'Antioch' hosta (*Hosta* 'Antioch')
13. Lady fern (*Athyrium filix-femina*)
14. 'Variegata Albida' violet (*Viola japonica* 'Variegata Albida')
15. Christmas rose (*Helleborus orientalis*)
16. Monkshood (*Aconitum napellus*)
17. 'The Rocket' ragwort (*Ligularia stenocephala* 'The Rocket')
18. Northern sea oats (*Chasmanthium latifolium*)
19. 'Snow Flurry' camellia (*Camellia* 'Snow Flurry')
20. 'Halcyon' hosta (*Hosta* 'Halcyon')
21. 'Peach Blossom' astilbe (*Astilbe* 'Peach Blossom')
22. 'Leucocarpa' inkberry (*Ilex glabra* 'Leucocarpa')
23. 'Alba' toad lily (*Tricyrtis hirta* 'Alba')
24. Japanese painted fern (*Athyrium nipponicum* var. *pictum*)

FOR ADDED INTEREST, YOU MAY ALSO WANT TO PLANT THESE BULBS:

'Frans Hals' dog-tooth violet (*Erythronium dens canis* 'Frans Hals')

'Citronella' dog-tooth violet (*Erythronium revolutum* 'Citronella')

'Blue Queen' Spanish bluebells (*Hyacinthoides hispanica* 'Blue Queen')

'White City' Spanish bluebells (*Hyacinthoides hispanica* 'White City')

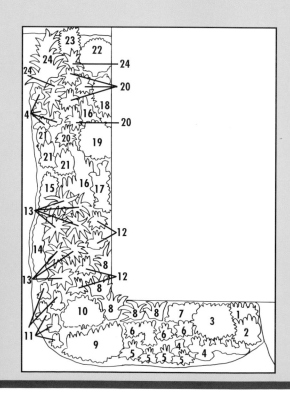

Sunny Cutting Garden Plant List

1. 'Minuet' Preston hybrid lilac (*Syringa prestoniae* 'Minuet')
2. 'Bressingham Bronze' alumroot (*Heuchera micrantha* 'Bressingham Bronze')
3. 'Lucifer' montbretia (*Crocosmia* 'Lucifer')
4. 'Summer Sun' false sunflower (*Heliopsis helianthoides* 'Summer Sun')
5. 'Black Knight' larkspur (*Delphinium* 'Black Knight')
6. 'Victoria' mealycup sage (*Salvia farinacea* 'Victoria')
7. 'William Penn' barberry (*Berberis* × *gladwynensis* 'William Penn')
8. Oriental fountain grass (*Pennisetum orientale*)
9. 'Blue Star' juniper (*Juniperus* 'Blue Star')
10. 'Compacta Plena' baby's breath (*Gypsophila paniculata* 'Compacta Plena')
11. 'Heavy Metal' blue switch grass (*Panicum virgatum* 'Heavy Metal')
12. 'David' summer phlox (*Phlox paniculata* 'David')
13. 'Provence' lavender (*Lavandula intermedia* 'Provence')
14. Jackman clematis (*Clematis jackmanii*)
15. 'Moonstone' peony (*Paeonia* 'Moonstone')
16. 'Frau Dagmar Hartopp' hybrid rugosa rose (*Rosa* 'Frau Dagmar Hartopp')
17. 'Snowbank' boltonia (*Boltonia asteroides* 'Snowbank')
18. 'Filagran' Russian sage (*Perovskia atriplicifolia* 'Filagran')
19. 'Sangria' lily (*Lilium* 'Sangria')
20. 'Perfecta Alba' pincushion flower (*Scabiosa caucasia* 'Perfecta Alba')
21. Love-in-a-mist (*Nigella damascena*)
22. 'Nesthackchen' New York aster (*Aster novi-belgii* 'Nesthackchen')
23. 'Conoy' Burkwood viburnum (*Viburnum* × *burkwoodii* 'Conoy')
24. 'Jewelberry' crab apple (*Malus* 'Jewelberry')

For additional seasonal interest, consider planting the following bulbs:

'Purple Sensation' ornamental onion (*Allium aflatunense* 'Purple Sensation')

'Camelot' daffodil (*Daffodil* 'Camelot')

'Kingsblood' tulip (*Tulipa* 'Kingsblood')

'Ballerina' tulip (*Tulipa* 'Ballerina')

'Ruiter Hybrids Mixed' foxtail lily (*Eremurus* 'Ruiter Hybrids Mixed')

'Blue Giant' garden hyacinth (*Hyacinthus* 'Blue Giant')

Formal Vegetable Garden

Following the tradition of eighteenth-century *potagers* in France, this vegetable garden takes a formal approach to growing culinary plants. To enhance its formal character, this garden features four separate planting beds separated by paths. While these paths are mown grass, the simplest to install, you may also create more formal walks with bricks set in a basketweave pattern.

Along the northern end of the garden is a low hedge, intended to provide a vista. Flanking the "gate" are terra-cotta pots with neatly clipped rosemary topiaries. The hedge of rugosa roses adds an ornamental touch and provides vitamin-rich rose hips come autumn.

Designed for an experienced and experimental cook, the garden is home to a wide array of vegetables and fruits. Many are kitchen staples while others—like okra, cilantro, lemongrass, and Chinese cabbage—are for specialized cooking. At the center of each bed is either a tripod for peas (with scarlet runner or other decorative beans following the peas) or a cage of plum or cherry tomatoes. The cages and tripods add height to the design scheme. This garden excludes large tomatoes, melons, squashes, and corn due to the ungainly and decidedly casual forms of these vegetables. Feel free to add your favorite vegetables to the mix, customizing the garden for your family's tastes.

The long, narrow pergola shaded by verdant grape vines features a bench centered on the east-west axis. This seat offers an escape from the strong summer sun, which is essential for growing vegetables and fruits but taxing for visitors to the garden. The pergola's six-foot (1.8m) width, when combined with the parallel four-foot (1.2m) perimeter path on that side of the garden, is just wide enough to accommodate a table and chairs for meals taken al fresco. A gate at the southern end of the pergola gives access to the kitchen door nearby.

Consider installing a fountain at the central circle of the garden, where the two garden axes meet. A two-tiered design adds height to the plan, while the sound of falling water is a soothing delight. The fountain can easily house a spigot for a convenient water source. If a fountain does not suit your taste or your budget, a large, stately urn can also serve as a suitable focal point.

With its rich variety of luscious vegetables and herbs and its careful, balanced design, this is a garden that offers a rare combination of beauty and practicality.

Tomatoes

INTENSIVE BEDS

Intensive planting with vegetables and herbs is a gardening method designed to reduce maintenance time while taking advantage of every inch of garden space. In this formal garden, vegetables and herbs are planted tightly.

As lettuces, cabbages, sorrel, early spinach, and beets are thinned or harvested, they leave room for growth of the remaining plants. And don't discard the thinnings—use them in salads and side dishes.

Intensive planting also reduces the space available for weeds, diminishing that tedious chore. To further reduce maintenance time, you might think about installing a timed watering system of drip hoses in each bed before the garden is planted.

STRETCHING THE SEASON

Part of the challenge in planting an extensive vegetable garden is planning for an abundance of harvest over a long period of time. By selecting different varieties with varying maturation rates, you can stretch the harvest season from late spring's earliest lettuces and peas to the hardy kales, cabbages, and chards that are ready to harvest in late autumn or even early winter. You'll find that a broad range of varietal choices is available for tomatoes, lettuce, fruit trees, beets, beans, broccoli, and peppers.

Planting beds intensively allows you to maximize garden space.

FORMAL VEGETABLE GARDEN PLANT LIST

1. Rosemary (*Rosmarinus officinalis*)
2. Pink rugosa rose (*Rosa rugosa*)
3. White rugosa rose (*Rosa rugosa*)
4. Marjoram (*Origanum majorana*)
5. Purple eggplant (*Solanum melongena* [choose a purple cultivar])
6. Compact basil (*Ocimum basilicum* 'Fino Verde Compatto')
7. Broccoli (*Brassica coleracea*, Botrytis Group)
8. Cherry tomato (*Lycopersicon lycopersicum* [choose a cherry-size cultivar])
9. White eggplant (*Solanum melongena* [choose a white cultivar])
10. Shallots (*Allium cepa*, Agregatum Group)
11. Lemongrass (*Cymbopogon citratus*)
12. Chives (*Allium schoenoprasum*)
13. Italian parsley (*Petroselinum neopolitanum*)
14. Red lettuce (*Lactuca sativa* [choose a red-leaved form])
15. Okra (*Abelmoschus esculentus*)
16. Plum tomato (*Lycopersicon lycopersicum* [choose a plum-type cultivar])
17. Dill (*Anethum graveolens*)
18. Chinese cabbage (*Brassica rapa*, Pekinensis Group)
19. Garlic (*Allium sativum*)
20. Sorrel (*Rumex acetosa*)
21. Bibb lettuce (*Lactuca sativa* [choose a Bibb form])
22. Cilantro (*Coriandrum sativum*)
23. Chamomile (*Matricaria recutita*)
24. Beet (*Beta vulgaris*, Crassa Group)
25. Chervil (*Anthriscus cerefolium*)
26. Bush cucumber (*Cucumis sativus* [choose a bush form])
27. Turnips (*Brassica rapa*, Rapifera Group)
28. Peas (*Pisum sativum*)
29. French tarragon (*Artemisia dracunculus* 'Sativa')
30. Bush beans (*Phaseolus vulgaris* [choose a bush form])
31. Scarlet runner bean (*Phaseolus coccineus*)
32. Thyme (*Thymus vulgaris*)
33. Green oregano (*Origanum heracleoticum*)
34. Red cabbage (*Brassica oleracea*, Capitata Group [choose a red form])
35. Kale (*Brassica oleracea*, Acephala Group)
36. Spinach (*Spinacia oleracea*)
37. Bronze fennel (*Foeniculum vulgare*)
38. Persian mint (*Mentha gattefosai*)
39. Summer savory (*Satureja hortensis*)
40. 'Concord' (deep purple), 'Catawba' (dark red), and 'Niagara' (light green to white) grapes (*Vitis* spp.)

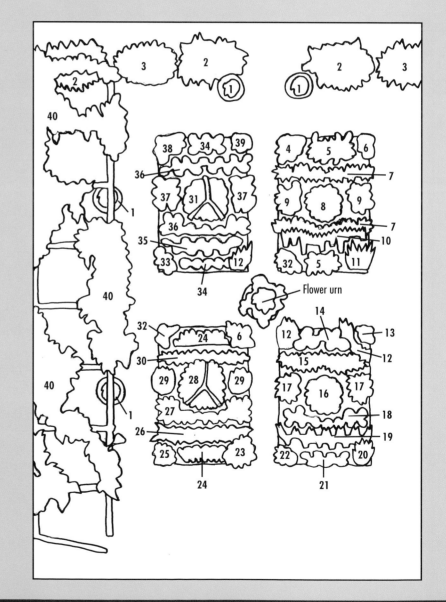

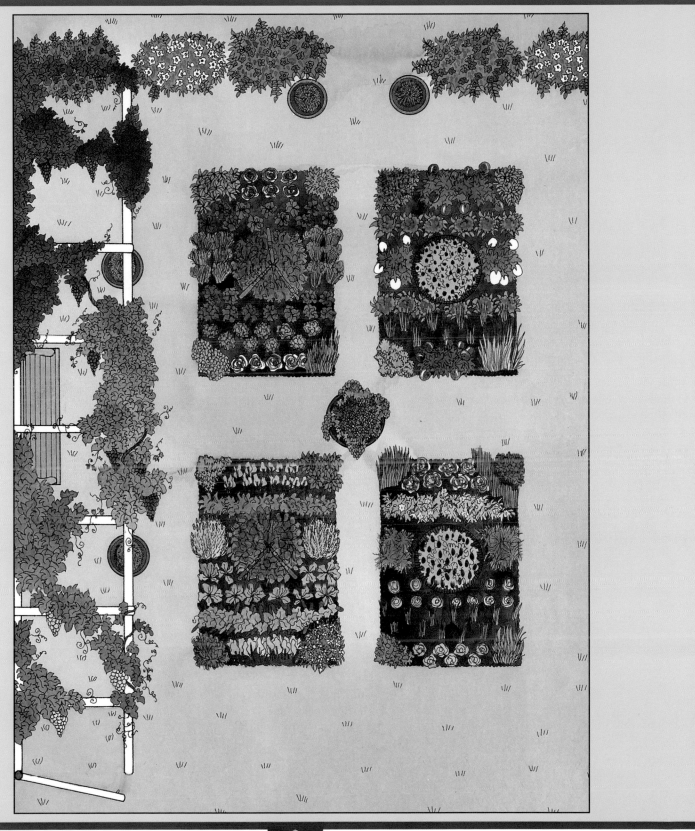

Ornamental Garden of Fruits

Some gardens have split personalities. An ornamental bed may be beautiful to behold while also providing a functional service, even if it is simply supplying bouquets of cut flowers. Plants grown for their appearance in the landscape may also be used to create dried flower crafts or fragrant potpourris, to add spice to culinary favorites, to attract butterflies, birds, or wildlife, or even to put food on the gardener's table. New breeds of compact, colorful vegetables are finding their way into perennial beds, while herbs are inching from the kitchen garden into the flower border. Fruiting trees are no longer restricted to orchards—some hybrids can even be grown in containers on a deck or patio! Fruiting shrubs for commercial use may still be planted in straight hillocks or rows, but for a small home garden, it is not unusual to find fruiting shrubs and perennials mixed in with plants of a more strictly ornamental variety.

Why go to the trouble of growing your own fruit when it is probably easier and possibly cheaper to purchase it at a store or farmer's market? One may as well ask "Why garden?" and be done with it. The reasons to grow your own fruit—or any sort of nourishment—are easy to enumerate: eating something you have grown yourself is fulfilling in a way that may hark back to our farming forebears; kids (or grown-ups!) who won't eat "store-bought" fruits will often be willing to munch on homegrown fruits right off the tree, shrub, vine, or plant; with heirloom seed sources, it is possible to grow tastier fruits of the past that are no longer available in stores; canning fruits and preserves can be much more economical than buying them at the store, and they certainly taste better; and because it is nice, in this age of processed nourishment, to make a connection with a food source in its natural form. There are a lot more reasons but those will do for a start.

Caring for fruiting plants requires slightly more involvement than caring for lower-maintenance ornamental plants, but a little effort will be richly rewarded by a fruitful harvest. First, be sure to plant in weed-free, loosely cultivated soil with shredded leaves, compost, or other organic matter worked in. Plant only to the soil line on the trunk or stem—planting too deeply could eventually kill the plant.

Leave sufficient room between plants—as much as six to eight feet (1.8 to 2.4m) for most fruiting shrubs, and even more for trees. Overcrowding eventually leads to restriction of air circulation as well as increased root competition, both of which can stress a plant and make it susceptible to disease and insect

Alpine strawberry blossoms

infestation. Apply mulch to a depth of about three inches (7cm) but leave a hollow well around the base of the trunk or stem. This helps route water directly to the root zone and reminds gardeners not to let mulch accumulate around the trunk.

Add a 10–10–10 starter fertilizer if you like (I prefer to wait a year before fertilizing trees, giving them a chance to become established first) and water deeply and frequently for at least the first few weeks. Once the plants are established, fertilize about every two weeks during the growing season, but do not overfertilize. Too much fertilizer will either burn the roots or promote the growth of foliage at the expense of fruits and flowers. On the other hand, trees and shrubs planted in soil that does not provide sufficient nutrients will be unlikely to fruit very heavily. A soil test early in the season will indicate whether fertilizer is needed, and, if so, in what proportions.

Granular fertilizers coated for slow release are preferable to liquid fertilizers in several ways, even though they do need to be watered in. For one thing, they only fertilize the area you want to be fertilized, unlike liquids, which can be carried by a breeze into neighboring plant beds and neighbors' yards. The slow-release formula is less likely to cause fertilizer burn and, because it is released over a period of weeks, fewer applications are required.

For a tree with fewer fruits—but of high quality—"thin" the fruits by removing a large quantity of the early crop when they are still quite small. Leave the best-looking fruits on the tree, with at least six inches (15cm) between each fruit. The remaining fruits will grow much larger and better-shaped than if they had been left crowded in bunches on the tree. Another word for the process of thinning fruit is "disbudding."

To help fruit trees bear the weight of heavy fruits, prune carefully to keep branches from getting overcrowded. It usually isn't necessary to do much pruning the first year, with a few exceptions: prune off any dead, diseased, or broken branches or roots before planting. Many experts recommended pruning off about a quarter of the root growth and a similar amount off the branches in order to stimulate new growth. I do not recommend removing branches from the top of the tree—especially not from the main trunk or "central leader"—but it can be helpful to prune back the branches a few inches. Cut at an angle to an outside bud; this will encourage new growth to branch outward instead of inward. Thin out crowded branches periodically, as well as crossed branches and branches that are growing at a very tight angle. Trees with a few strong branches, spaced with several inches separating them, will be most able to support heavy fruit growth.

Fruiting trees and shrubs are susceptible to a certain number of pests and diseases; these will not be totally eliminated even if you plant resistant varieties. Keep an eye out for problems and consult your Agricultural Extension Service for a diagnosis and recommended treatment as soon as you suspect a problem may exist.

Highbush blueberries

FRUITS FOR A CONTAINER GARDEN

Small fruiting plants such as strawberries have long been grown in containers and pots, but it is also possible to grow some fruiting trees and shrubs in containers. Use a sturdy, fairly large container such as a wooden half-barrel, and drill quite a few small holes in the base and around the sides to ensure sufficient drainage. Prepare a planting mix with potting soil, peat moss, compost, or organic matter such as shredded leaves, as well as a little sand or vermiculite to keep the mix from getting too dense and heavy. You may want to add a cup or two of water-retaining polymers to ensure that the roots don't dry out. (Don't overdo it, though—polymer crystals swell up like globs of Jell-O when watered.)

Fill the container about one third full of the potting mix, then set the tree or shrub on top of the soil, spreading the roots out. (If the plant is bareroot, soak the roots in a bucket of water overnight prior to planting.) Carefully add the rest of the soil, patting it down around the roots and holding the plant upright in the center of the container. Add soil until it levels off at the place on the trunk or stem that indicates the depth where it was planted at the nursery. Do not set the plant too deeply in the soil. (Tomatoes, also considered a fruit, are an exception—pull off a few of the lower leaves and bury the roots and lower part of the stem in the soil. Additional roots will form where the leaves were removed.)

Leave some space at the top of the container so the soil will not overflow when watered. Add mulch, just as you would in the garden, and underplant with annuals if you like. Some mat-forming groundcovers can be planted in containers but be cautious when underplanting shrubs or trees in containers with perennials. There is no place for the roots to spread and if there is too much competition for air, water, and nutrients, none of the containerized plants will thrive.

Colonnade apple trees produced by Stark Bro's grow eight feet tall by only two feet wide and are well suited for container planting; in order to produce fruit, two varieties are needed to ensure pollination. 'Garden Delicious' is a self-pollinating extra dwarf apple available from Burpee; it grows only five to six feet [1.5 to1.8m] tall and produces yellow apples that flush with red in cooler climates. Burpee also offers 'Garden Sun' peach trees and 'Golden Prolific' nectarines in extra dwarf varieties suitable for container planting; each plant grows four to five feet [1.2 to 1.5cm] tall. Stark Bro's offers a range of miniature fruit trees suitable for container planting; they will grow only four to eight feet [1.2 to 2.4m] tall. The miniatures include: Stark Sensation peach, Stark GoldenGlo apricot, Stark HoneyGlo nectarine, Stark Jon-A-Red Jonathan apple, and Stark Golden Delicious apple. Container fruit trees are generally hardy in zones 5 to 8; zone 4 with protection.

Apples

Ornamental Garden of Fruits
Plant List

1. Blackhaw viburnum (*Viburnum prunifolium*)
2. 'Forest Prince' apple serviceberry (*Amelanchier ×
   grandiflora* 'Forest Prince'; in Canada, serviceberries are called "saskatoons.")
3. Highbush blueberries (*Vaccinium corymbosum*;
   plant at least two varieties for best fruit set:
   'Blueray', 'Bluejay', 'Elliott', 'Northland', or
   dwarf cultivars such as 'Friendship' and 'Dwarf
   Northblue'.)
4. Compact American cranberrybush viburnum
   (*Viburnum trilobum* 'Compactum')
5. 'Mount Royal' dwarf European plum (*Prunus ×
   'Mount Royal'*)
6. Jonathan apple (*Malus* × Stark 'Jon-A-Red')
7. 'Golden Prolific' nectarine (*Prunus* × 'Golden
   Prolific')
8. 'Stark Sensation' peach (*Prunus* × 'Stark
   Sensation')
9. Wild rose (*Rosa rubrifolia*)
10. 'Rubra' rugosa rose (*Rosa rugosa* 'Rubra')
11. Alpine strawberries (*Fragaria* × 'Improved
    Rugens')
12. Wild strawberries or fraises du bois (*Fragaria vesca*
    'Semperflorens')

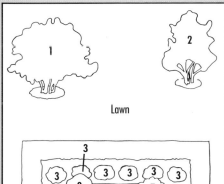

Low-Maintenance Garden

There is a popular myth, cultivated by some retailers anxious to make a sale, that it is possible to have a no-maintenance garden. It is easy to fall for that kind of sales pitch when confronted in the garden center with an array of vivid flowers and rows of vibrantly healthy shrubs. It is a little harder to believe when the plants are lined up in your driveway, waiting for someone to dig big holes in 80°F [27°C] heat. At some point even the most innocent beginning gardener is forced to admit it: there is no such thing as a no-maintenance garden.

On the other hand, a *low-maintenance* garden is certainly possible, and is not even that difficult to prepare. The bulk of the preparation will take place before the plants have even been purchased. Selecting a site is the first priority—you may have your heart set on an island bed smack in the middle of the front yard, but stop and consider the site before you start to dig. Is the prospective site in full sun or deep shade? Neither of those conditions is ideal for a low-maintenance garden. A partially sunny spot in the filtered shade of a thornless honey locust won't need as much watering as a completely unshaded spot. A garden planted in full shade can certainly thrive, given attention and appropriate plant material, but a garden in dappled shade will be far less demanding.

'Autumn Joy' stonecrop

Before you plant is also the best time to test the soil pH and make any amendments necessary to bring the soil to optimum health. Work shredded leaves and properly prepared and aged compost into the soil before planting—it is a lot easier to improve the soil before the plants are installed than to fix soil problems later. For best results, send a few soil samples to an accredited testing lab (this can often be done through your local agricultural extension agent). The results of the soil test will indicate the levels of necessary nutrients present in the soil as well as the availability of those nutrients. In a badly compacted soil with poor air and water circulation, plants may not be able to get at nutrients even if they are present in the required amounts.

It is generally not necessary to fertilize newly planted flowers, trees, or shrubs, although many people swear by 10–10–10 starter fertilizers. With trees and shrubs, I prefer to wait until they have had a year to become established before applying fertilizer. With perennials and annuals, I apply fertilizer about every two weeks until the middle of July. Be careful with popular foliar feeders—they are high in nitrogen, which can give you lush green foliage at the expense of flowers. I learned this the hard way, with a border of marigolds so tall and dense they looked like a hedge and only a

few flowers to brighten the effect. Roses are heavy feeders that need both frequent watering and fertilizing, but I would hesitate to include roses in a garden planted for low maintenance.

Once the site is selected and the soil prepared, it is time to decide which plants to include in the garden. A little research will help narrow down the plant list: first, check with gardening friends or local experts (master gardeners, the staff of botanic gardens, or agricultural extension agents) to find out which plants perform well in your area. Experimenting is fun, but can be risky if you are trying to stress low maintenance.

Once you have a short list of recommended regional plants, eliminate any that you don't like or that have a tendency to spread rapidly. If the plants will need staking, cross them off your list. If they are prone to insect or disease problems, strike them out. If a plant you really want to have in your garden is notorious for problems of these kinds, check a little further. While certain species of plants are known for their propensity to disease, tendency to spread, or for their shaggy

appearance, there may be new, improved hybrids that eliminate these problems.

At the top of the list should be plants that are drought- and heat-tolerant, plants that will survive any extreme weather conditions in your area, those that maintain good form without pruning and that will remain compact in size, and plants that have a long period of bloom. Be sure to include a few species with handsome foliage that will keep the garden interesting when the peak bloom time is past. An underplanting of bulbs can extend the season of interest, but stick to small bulbs like grape hyacinths. These will eventually form clumps of color, but they do not require the after-care (such as tying back the dying foliage) of daffodils and they are not as fussy as tulips. Ornamental grasses can provide autumn and winter interest, and while it may be beneficial to cut back the dead foliage in spring, it is not absolutely necessary.

Once your plants are selected and purchased, plant them immediately—dig a hole twice as wide as the root ball but only as deep as it was previously planted. The exceptions are peonies (which are best planted with the eye one inch (2.5cm) below the soil) and tubers or bulbs, which have varying ideal planting depths. Do not plant in the heat of the day if you can avoid it—early in the morning or overcast days are a better choice. Water the plants well until they are established—even the most drought-tolerant plants need water after they have been transplanted.

Treat yourself and your garden to a layer of mulch about three inches (7cm) thick, being careful not to mound up the mulch too deeply or too close to the plants. Water well before applying the mulch. I don't recommend using black plastic in your garden because it is unsightly and takes a long time to break down. Instead of putting plastic under volcanic rock, mulch, or marble chips, try a thick layer of newspapers instead.

Mulch is available in many forms, with a wide range of prices. Most finely shredded bark mulches are effective in holding back weeds if applied to a uniform depth of about three inches (7cm). In addition to weed control, mulch will help keep the soil evenly moist, protect the plants from extremes of weather, and keep the soil temperature fairly uniform. Virtually any mulch is going to need topping up in future years, but that effort is more than paid for by the benefits of mulch.

By mulching to control weeds and selecting plants carefully to eliminate frequent pruning and pest problems, you can keep common maintenance tasks to a minimum. Deadhead plants when you get a chance—it makes them look neater and can bring on another flush of flowering. Water and fertilize as needed, and watch for early signs of pest and disease problems so they can be treated quickly. Even weekend gardeners should be able to handle the demands of a garden especially designed for its low-maintenance requirements.

RING AROUND THE ROSY

An easy way to create a very small, exceptionally easy-to-maintain garden is also beneficial for existing trees and shrubs. Simply cut away a circle of sod from existing trees or shrubs, creating a "tree circle." Don't be stingy—if the tree is large, cut away the sod all the way to the drip line (as far as the leaves extend). Work the soil lightly, with a fork rather than a spade, so that you don't damage the roots. Tree roots extend much wider—sometimes as much as fifty feet (15m) or more—than most people think, and are much less deep. Many roots are close to the surface of the soil, even in mature trees, so take care to disturb the soil as little as possible. Add topsoil if necessary, but sparingly—if the grade or level of the soil is changed, the tree could die.

Shrubs and roses will also benefit from tree circles, since grass competes with their roots for air, water, and nutrients in the soil. When planting inside a tree ring, select annuals that will grow in the shade of the existing plant or tree or try shallow-rooted perennials that will not create damaging root competition. Roses in particular are not fond of competition, although some herbs and companion plants are known to discourage rose pests. Water and fertilize as needed, but do not apply herbicides in any form, since they can kill the existing plant or tree.

Install a shredded bark mulch to a depth of about three inches (7cm), extending the mulch to the end of the tree ring. Do not allow the mulch to mound up close to tree trunks or the base of shrubs—it creates a hiding place for damaging rodents and can cause the base of the trunk to rot. Form a hollow crater around the base of the existing tree or shrub—it will help water funnel directly to the roots while keeping the mulch at a safe distance. Simply spade the edge of the tree ring periodically to keep grass from invading—wood, metal, and plastic edging can heave out of the soil. This edging is often an added expense that can end up making the tree ring look messy rather than neat. A sharply spaded edge is very effective and all it costs is a few minutes of labor.

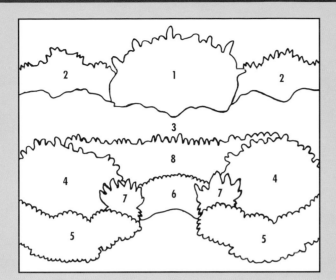

LOW-MAINTENANCE GARDEN
PLANT LIST

1. 'Royal Purple' purple smokebush (*Cotinus coggygria* 'Royal Purple')
2. 'Magnus' purple coneflower (*Echinacea purpurea* 'Magnus')
3. 'Autumn Joy' stonecrop (*Hylotelephium* × 'Autumn Joy' [formerly *Sedum* × 'Autumn Joy'])
4. Globe blue spruce (*Picea pungens* 'Glauca Globosa')
5. 'Crimson Pigmy' barberry (*Berberis thunbergii* 'Crimson Pigmy')
6. 'Ralph Shugert' periwinkle (*Vinca minor* 'Ralph Shugert')
7. 'Purple Palace' alumroot (*Heuchera micrantha* 'Purple Palace')
8. 'Sunny Border Blue' speedwell (*Veronica* × 'Sunny Border Blue')

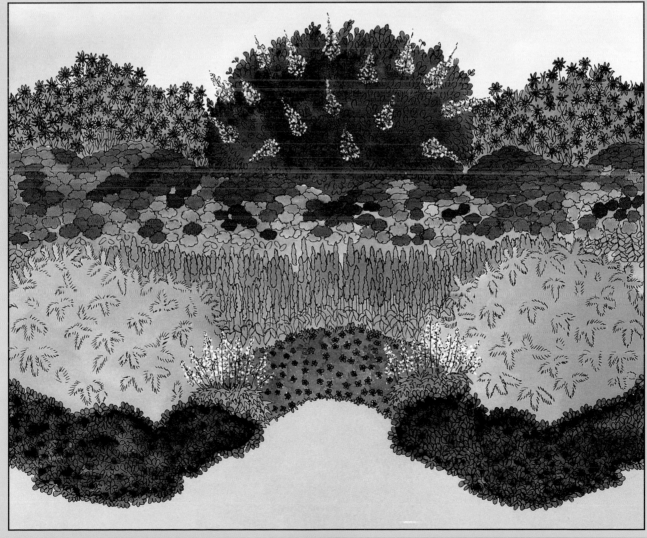

Sources

W. Atlee Burpee and Company
Warminster, PA 18974

Bear Creek Nursery
PO Box 411
Northport, WA 99157

Benner's Gardens
6974 Upper York Road
New Hope, PA 18938

Busse Gardens
Route 2, Box 238
Cokato, MN 55321

Carrol Gardens
444 East Main Street
Westminster, MD 21157

Comstock Seed
8520 W. 4th St.
Reno, NV 89523

The Daffodil Mart
7463 Heath Trail
Gloucester, VA 2306

Edible Landscaping
PO Box 77
Afton, VA 22920

Finch Blueberry Nursery
PO Box 699
Bailey, NC 27807

Forestfarm
990 Tetherow Road
Williams, OR 97544

The Fragrant Path
PO Box 328
Ft. Calhoun, NE 68023

Gardens of the Blue Ridge
9056 Pittman Gap Road
PO Box 10
Pineola, NC 28662

Greenlee Nursery
301 Franklin Avenue
Pomona, CA 91766

Greer Gardens
1280 Goodpasture Island
Eugene,OR 97401-1794

Heronswood Nursery Ltd.
7503 NE 288th Street
Kingston, WA 98346-9502

Holbrook Farm & Nursery
115 Lance Road
PO Box 368
Fletcher, NC 28732

Jackson & Perkins
PO Box 1028
Medford, OR 97501

Kurt Bluemel, Inc.
2740 Green Lane
Baldwin, MD 21013-9523

Lilypons Water Gardens
PO Box 10
6800 Lilypons Road
Buckeystown, MD 21717

Logee's Greenhouses, Ltd.
141 North Street
Danielson, CT 06239-1939

McClure and Zimmerman
PO Box 358
108 W. Winnebago Street
Friesland, WI 53935

Niche Gardens
1111 Dawson Road
Chapel Hill, NC 27516

Park Seed
1 Parkton Avenue
Greenwood, SC 29647-0001

Pen Y Bryn Nursery
1 Box 1313
Forksville, PA 18616

Plant Delights Nursery, Inc.
9241 Sauls Road
Raleigh, NC 27603

Prairie Moon Nursery
Rt. 3 Box 163
Winona, MN 55987

Prairie Nursery
PO Box 306
Westfield, WI 53964

Roslyn Nursery
211 Burrs Lane
Dix Hills, NY 11746

The Sandy Mush Herb Nursery
316 Surrett Cove Road
Leicester, North Carolina 28748-9622

Shady Oaks Nursery
112 10th Ave. SE
Waseca, MN 56093

Shepherd's Garden Seeds
30 Irene Street
Torrington, CT 06790

Shooting Star Nursery
444 Bates Road
Frankfort, KY 40601

Thompson and Morgan Inc.
PO Box 1308
Jackson, NJ 08527-0308

Tripple Brook Farm
37 Middle Rd.
Southampton, MA 01073

Van Engelen Inc.
23 Tulip Drive
Bantam, CT 06750

Van Ness Water Gardens
2460 N. Euclid Ave.
Upland, CA 91786

Vermont Wildflower Farm
Rt. 7
Charlotte, VT 05445

Wayside Gardens
Garden Lane
Hodges, SC 29695

Westgate Garden Nursery
751 Westgate Drive
Eureka, CA 95503

Wildwood Gardens
14488 Rock Creek Road
Chardon, OH 44024

White Flower Farm
PO Box 50
Litchfield, CT 06759

CANADA

Corn Hill Nursery Ltd.
RR 5
Petitcodiac NB EOA 2HO

Ferncliff Gardens
SS 1
Mission, British Columbia
V2V 5V6

Morden Nurseries, Ltd.
PO Box 1270
Morden, MB
Canada R0G 1J0

McFayden Seed Co. Ltd.
Box 1800
Brandon, Manitoba
R7A 6N4

Stirling Perennials
RR 1
Morpeth, Ontario
N0P 1X0

AUSTRALIA

Country Farm Perennials
RSD Laings Road
Nayook VIC 3821

Cox's Nursery
RMB 216 Oaks Road
Thrilmere NSW 2572

Honeysuckle Cottage Nursery
Lot 35 Bowen Mountain Road
Bowen Mountain via Grosevale
NSW 2753

Index

PHOTOGRAPHY CREDITS

©David Cavagnaro: pp. 37, 49, 58, 65, 72, 90, 99, 108

©R. Todd Davis: pp. 18, 20, 22, 45 bottom, 48, 52, 62, 64, 73, 76, 87

©Derek Fell: pp. 36, 86

©John Glover: pp. 29, 57, 60, 66, 78, 83, 84, 94, 104, 105, 109, 110

©Dency Kane: pp. 11, 24, 28, 32, 38, 42, 43, 53, 56, 61, 79, 82, 98, 100, 101 112, 113

©Charles Mann: pp. 12, 13, 14, 19, 23, 40, 45 top, 54, 68, 69, 88, 95

©Jerry Pavia: 15, 77

ILLUSTRATIONS

Line Art: Amy Talluto

Color Art: ©Jane Kendall